AMERICA THE POLICE STATE

WHY AND HOW TO FIX USA

By Roger K. Daneth

Copyright 2018 Roger K. Daneth, all rights reserved.

Preface

In publishing this book there is no intent to incite discontent in America, and I do not advocate any change to our Constitution, or our form of government. My intent only is to point out where some laws, judicial practices, and police methods used in America should be corrected before America starts down a path towards a police state or even possibly a totalitarian form of government.
I believe in the U.S. Constitution where it says "...all men are created equal..." and I believe that all men should be treated equally under the law

without discrimination based on race, creed, or color.

In this book I first describe what I think are our problems that are pulling us towards a police state, and then I proceed to present solutions that some people have already pointed to, and ones that I myself are proposing.

When you read this book you may agree with little if anything of what I propose as solutions, but the facts of the problems are documented by various sources of information that are provided in each case. Whatever suppositions I have made in this book will only be because of a lack of data on certain subjects. It is my goal to avoid such suppositions and try to support all statements of substance with factual data in a fair and impartial manner.

Introduction

America is a democracy and one of the most freedom loving countries in the world. We have one of the best economies and many great companies and institutions. We have excellent medical and health systems. Our technical achievements and military power exceed that of any country in the world. Many good and great things have been done by Americans for Americans and other peoples of the world. There is almost no end to America's great achievements.

But in America we do have some problems. We have a drug problem. We have a crime problem. We have the highest number of people incarcerated of any country in the world. We have an education problem. We have people who cannot get jobs. We have discrimination of every type. We suffer from political correctness gone mad. We suffer from excessive taxation of business. Our infrastructure is in decay. Our money is losing its value. Our politicians spend most of their time fighting each other and wasting taxpayer's money. Our police are trying to function with inadequate budgets and manpower in the face of increasing crime in the streets.

In this book, I will draw your attention to the crime problem, its root causes, and possible solutions. I hope that Americans will find this book to be helpful, in the right spirit of bringing lawful changes, and improving the plight of the poor and disadvantaged people of our country.

Chapter 1
Discrimination, police power and brutality

America is now in the first stage of a possible development into a full- fledged police state. If you doubt this just consider the facts that I describe below. There are a number of forces that are moving us in the direction of a police state. These forces are intertwined and working together in a powerful and sinister way to increase the power of the police and erode our constitutional freedoms.

The rise of the power of the executive branch and the Department of Justice at the expense of Congress is a threat to our democratic form of government and could pave the way to a police state dictatorship, if the power of the executive branch continues to grow along with the growing power of local police jurisdictions.

The discrimination against African-Americans is still present in the U.S. and results in their segregation, unemployment, and many living a life of poverty. Those who do find jobs only have low paying jobs such as in fast-food chains or the large discount retail stores. Joblessness and low pay for people who do find work leads to a life of crime for young men.

The opportunity for young African-Americans to get a good education is very limited because of the low income or impoverished condition of their family. Those who do get a good education may still find it hard to get a good paying job because of the tendency for discrimination in favor of white or Caucasian graduates. Lately studies have shown that the best jobs in "Silicon Valley" large corporations are heavily occupied by white men with few minorities and women in the higher paying positions.

How many police does the USA have?

USA already has more than 780,000 police, and is third in number behind China and India with much larger populations. Why are there so many police in the U.S.? The large number of police stems from Richard Nixon's "War on Drugs" mainly, but also because of the number of the arrests and prosecutions for petty crimes that result from foolish laws and regulations promulgated by politicians and "do-gooders" who frown on any kind of activity that they deem to be undesirable or obnoxious.

In order to roll-back the number of police we need to stop arresting everyone for minor "offenses". The more laws there are that generate more "crime" incidents, the more police that are required to enforce the ridiculous laws and regulations.

The increasing numbers of police are also generated by the increasing crime that results from the increasing poverty and joblessness in the ranks of minorities in America. American cities now have vast "slum" neighborhoods where gangs, drugs, robbery, drive-by shootings, and general lawlessness prevail. What are the main generators of the problems? The crime problem is due to several things combining to work against people. These are discrimination, the "War on Drugs", poor education, and as I detail below bad government policies that shackle businesses, and reduce the number of good paying jobs available.

See link A for police numbers per country.

Link A: http://en.wikipedia.org/wiki/List_of_countries_by_number_of_police_officers

Just the sheer number of police per capita relative to other countries is a major problem in itself. The more police there are, the greater their cumulative joint power will be through their interconnected network of information exchange and the sheer force of numbers.

Lately police in some larger communities have taken to using military equipment and tactics. Once the American police forces become virtually fully militarized, the population will be at the mercy of their unbeatable force and their leadership. If their leadership becomes the willing lackeys of unscrupulous politicians who control the federal and state governments, we may find that our U.S. Constitution has been bypassed or relegated to the trash bin. Then our country will be in the iron grip of despots and the militarized police forces.

If you think this cannot happen, let history become your guide. Consider what happened before the start of the Second World War when first Russia came under the communist boots and then Germany, Japan, and Italy were taken over and turned into the fascist police states that America had to fight at terrible cost.

Then remember the iron grip that the KGB police had on the Russian population? Did that change by the population rising up against them? No, Russia did not change until some more reasonable men came into power. Now again, Russia is controlled by a dictator and his police lackeys.

Consider also the communist states of North Korea, China, and Cuba. These states are under the control of the dictatorship of the communist party supported by massive police forces. There is no democracy in these states and there is little possibility of the people ever becoming free under democratic leadership, not matter how many "free trade" agreements the U.S. signs, and no matter how much the U.S. "negotiates" with these countries.

Over many decades, and with different presidents in office, the power of the executive branch has grown at the expense of the U.S. Congress. Bills passed by the Congress are routinely vetoed by the executive branch. Unfortunately, the Supreme Court has been "packed" by presidents with people who are politically aligned with the president's politics, whether Republican or Democrat. The effect is that the combined power of the executive branch and the judicial branch overwhelm the legislative branch, so that the executive branch is essentially ruling the country. Laws that do manage to pass without a veto may be struck down by the Supreme Court on as "unconstitutional" or on some other legal technicality.

Of course the U.S. Congress does have the power to confirm or reject presidential appointments to the Supreme Court, and it needs to exercise this power very carefully to make sure that candidates are unbiased in terms of their political beliefs and in other matters such as race or religion.

If executive power is in control of the Justice Department, then the federal law enforcement agencies, such as the FBI, the Bureau Alcohol, Tobacco, and Firearms, the Federal Marshals, the Environmental Protection Agency, the IRS, OSHA, and others, become very powerful and they are able to apply police force under executive fiat. America then becomes the consummate police state, and the people are at the mercy of the executive branch of government. Again Congress should make sure that the person appointed to the position of Attorney General will not be a political puppet of the executive branch, so that the Justice Department will be as independent as possible from the executive branch.

Discrimination

Racial and other forms of discrimination are some of the biggest problems in America and are one of the root causes of poverty and the crime problem. Although there has been a lot of progress, people are still faced with problems getting jobs and respect in America because of their sex, race, religion, appearance, age, culture, or nationality.

Discrimination is one of the main reasons certain groups are largely poor and disadvantaged. The playing field is not level. If you do not fit a certain "profile" you will have trouble getting a job, borrowing money, getting in the best schools, etc., no matter how good your credentials are. The list goes on.

At the present time the African American population is still suffering from police brutality, poverty due to poor education, and residential segregation. All of these factors put African Americans at a big disadvantage when competing with the white population for jobs and a path for equality and growth in society.

Also the growing Hispanic segment of America has similar problems competing with whites for good paying jobs.

Discrimination is one of the forces driving America towards a police state

How does this apply to America becoming a police state? The reason is that when millions of young men and women cannot find work because they do not fit an employer's "profile" of what he thinks will make a good worker, these young people may give up looking for a legal job and turn to crime as a way to survive. So that is a major reason for crimes like burglary, robbery, drug dealing, and other criminal activities.

In a white dominated business environment people of color are rarely hired for the better paying jobs and they will find that they are likely to be by-passed for raises and promotions in favor of the white workers, especially if the business is operated by "good ol' boy" system where unless you are part of the clique of "white boys" in the business, you cannot expect to get promoted or get the good jobs.

Yes, discrimination is not always obvious or overt, but it is still there in many areas of the country and in many businesses.

The so-called "affirmative action" plan adopted by some organizations has been helpful in some instances but there are still underlying attitudes and maybe even unconscious motives that result in discrimination that are just as real today as it was in the past.

Discrimination can happen to anyone in America

How does a white man get discriminated against you might wonder? For example, he might not fit a "profile" of an employer just based on his appearance being a little out of the average appearance of a white man. Maybe he is very tall, or overweight, has a long beard, or is over the age of 50 or 60. Whatever the reason is, he is being discriminated against. The same types of discrimination apply to other races and cultures in America also.

What is the solution? I will write more on this subject below.

Police killings and brutality

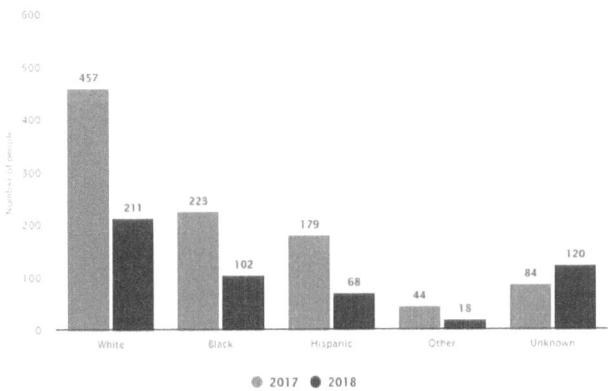

The number of people shot to death by police from 2017 through June 2018 by race.

In 2017 to June of 2018, 668 white men were shot by police compared to 325 black men. Blacks are only 13% of the population so this shows the unequal high proportion of black people that are shot by police compared to white people!

Nearly twice a week during a seven year period ending in 2012, a white police officer killed a black person, according to the *USA Today* report titled "Local police involved in 400 killings per year", reported by Carly Mallenbaum, Kevin Johnson, Meghan Hoyer, and Brad Heath of *USA Today* , on August 15, 2014. See link no. 1.

Link no. 1
http://www.usatoday.com/story/news/nation/2014/08/14/police-killings-data/14060357/

Approximately 400 people are killed yearly by police in USA according to the article and this number is thought to be incomplete because not all police jurisdictions participate in the reporting, according to the article.

In 2012-2014 we had exceptionally bad cases of black men being shot to death, the Trayvon Martin case, the Michael Brown case, the Eric Garner case, and the Rumain Brisbon shooting. See Links, 1A, 1B, 1C, 1D. Also see link 1E that has a list of police brutality going back to 1951 in various states of America.
Links 1F and 1G show that there are also black-on-white crimes, and police brutality against whites, respectively. Link 1H tells us the dangerous side of law enforcement with statistics on officers who have been killed in the line of duty.

The Trayvon Martin Case

Trayvon Martin was shot on February 6th, 2012, not by a police officer but by a self-styled community watch volunteer, George Zimmerman. The case is not a clear-cut murder because of the evidence of injuries to George Zimmerman indicating that a struggle had occurred. Mr. Zimmerman eventually went to trial but he was acquitted of murder based on the Florida "stand your ground" law and other evidence.

The case had overtones of racism and was possibly caused by a clash of two different cultures. Mr. Zimmerman perceived Trayvon as one of the "bad guys" to be followed and possibly harassed by Mr. Zimmerman, while Trayvon perhaps resented the harassment by Zimmerman and a scuffle resulted, causing Zimmerman to shoot Trayvon, even though Trayvon was not armed.

I am including this case because it is an example of the violent and deadly results that occur because of racism in America. See link 1A for a complete history of the case.

Link 1A
http://en.wikipedia.org/wiki/Trayvon_Martin

The Michael Brown Shooting

Michael Brown, and unarmed teenager, was shot by a Ferguson Mo. policeman on August 9th of 2014. This is a very sad case of an encounter between a teenager suspected of a robbery and an inept or relatively inexperienced policeman. Briefly, Michael Brown was stopped by the policeman and a struggle for the policeman's gun ensued, ending in an altercation with multiple gunshot wounds on the teenager, resulting in his death.

Unfortunately, there were conflicting witnesses that caused confusion as to whether the death was in self-defense, or a homicide, on the part of the policeman.

A Grand Jury decided to acquit the policeman of any wrong doing. After the verdict, riots, looting, and destruction of property followed. The police reacted poorly, failing to control the crowd and failing to protect property.

This incident is an example of a problem with police training and tactics that caused deadly harm to a young person, and destruction of property and businesses.

The details are well documented by *Wikipedia* at link 1B.

Link 1B
http://en.wikipedia.org/wiki/Shooting_of_Michael_Brown

Protests have continued as I am writing this book. On March 11, 2015, two Ferguson Missouri policemen were shot and critically wounded during an evening protest. The policemen survived and a massive manhunt for the shooter took place. An excellent article and video was published by *Reuter's* news service written by Kate Munsch, titled "Ambush of policemen triggers manhunt in racially tense Ferguson". See link 1B-2.

Link 1B-2:
http://www.reuters.com/article/2015/03/12/us-usa-missouri-shooting-protest-idUSKBN0M80CJ20150312

The Eric Garner killing

The killing of Eric Garner on July 17th, 2014 is also a very sad case of the killing of an individual who had committed no violent crime. In this case, however, there is a video that shows the arrest of Eric Garner and the horrific results that followed.

A policeman grabbed Eric from behind with a hold alleged to be similar to a "choke-hold", or an actual choke-hold. to take Eric down to the pavement. Eric repeatedly said that he could not breathe, but the policeman would not release his grip until it was too late, and Eric was mortally wounded.

The choke-hold is prohibited by the New York Police Department rules. So why was a deadly hold allegedly used on a suspect of a non-violent crime? Supposedly, Eric was resisting arrest. But the video does not show that Eric was violent in any way during the arrest.

He may have been *protesting* his arrest, but is this a reason to use a violent choke-hold and take down of a non-violent criminal? It seems that the police need better non-lethal tactics, and less violent tactics to deal with simple non-violent protesting of an arrest!

The police definitely acted stupidly in this case. Was it because of a lack of training, or is it an attitude problem that the NYPD has against minorities?

The Grand Jury returned a verdict of "not guilty" against the police officer that perpetrated the alleged choke-hold. Peaceful demonstrations occurred on the night of December 4th, 2014. Unfortunately, a lot of people were arrested, even though their demonstration was peaceful. Did this action by the police help to foster community trust and harmony? I don't believe that it did. This case is a prime example of lethal police mayhem that is characteristic of a police state!

America, you should be aware of the road we are on towards the formation of an onerous police state, instead of the democracy that our founding fathers tried to establish for us.

Eric Garner was only trying to make some income by selling cigarettes that did not have the New York City tax stamp on them. People bring in cigarettes from New Jersey or other towns that do not have the high New York City tax applied and sell them for a profit. It is a small black market that was created by New York City when they added the excessively high tax for sales inside the city. The high tax is like making cigarettes illegal for all practical purposes-- essentially creating another situation where more police are needed to control the traffic in illegal cigarette sales.

The Eric Garner killing was documented by *Wikipedia* also. See link 1C.

Link 1C
http://en.wikipedia.org/wiki/Death_of_Eric_Garner

The Rumain Brisbon shooting on December 4th of 2014

The Rumain Brisbon shooting is another case of the police acting stupidly by shooting an unarmed man. I am citing this case for several reasons:

a) The policeman who shot Rumain was acting stupidly with premature haste and failure to properly asses the situation before fatally shooting an unarmed man.

b) Rumain was a non-violent drug dealer. We do not know why he decided to be a drug dealer, but it is probably because the lure of the money to be made was great, and it was hard for him to find a decent job that pays a reasonable wage (due to a number of factors such as discrimination against minorities, poor public education, and a lack of jobs for people who do not have special skills, or advanced training of some type.)

c) The laws have created a black market for drugs, thereby creating opportunities for criminals to deal drugs for a living. It is a similar situation to the Prohibition era of the 20's and early 30's when illegal liquor was made and distributed by criminals operating in the black market created by the Prohibition law.

As I am writing this, there is not a lot of information available in the news about Rumain, except some praise from a friend, and an accusation of a police cover-up.
Brisbon did have a non-violent criminal record, but whether Rumain was a good man or not, is not the issue. The issue is that he did not deserve to die for a non-violent crime at the hands of an obviously inept policeman! See the *Huff Post's* article "Rumain Brisbon's Friend Disputes Phoenix Police Account of Killing", by Michael McLaughlin, dated December 10, 2014. See link 1D1.

Link 1D1
http://www.huffingtonpost.com/2014/12/05/rumain-brisbon-phoenix-police_n_6278966.html

But don't miss-understand. I do not condone law breaking. But I do question laws that cause non-violent criminals to be sent to prison, and create black markets that tempt people with the large quantities of money that can be made operating in black markets. And I do question the use of deadly force in non-violent crime cases when the suspect is not even armed! See the article "Phoenix Police Shoot Unarmed Black Man, Igniting Outcry", in the *Huff Post* of December 10, 2014, by AP's Terry Tang.

   See Link 1D2.

Link 1D2
http://www.huffingtonpost.com/2014/12/04/phoenix-police-shooting_n_6273278.html

The case of Tamir Rice, a 12 year old shot by Cleveland police

Tamir Rice was a young black child only 12 years old who was playing in a park with a toy pistol. Unfortunately, the toy pistol looked like a real weapon. Someone called police that a *boy* with a gun was in the park. The 911 operator apparently did not mention that the boy was a *boy* when the police were informed.
The police arrived on the scene and shot the boy who died of the gunshot wound. Now, yes, maybe the boy should not have been playing with the realistic looking weapon, and yes, *such toys should be illegal,* but in any case the boy died because of apparent poor police procedure or

training. This is a very sad case that should be a wake-up call for all Americans concerning the need for better police qualification standards, procedures, and training of policemen.

A Washington Post article titled " Death of Tamir Rice, 12-year-old shot by Cleveland police, ruled a homicide", by Abby Ohlheiser shows a copy of the autopsy report, and describes the incident in detail.

See link 1D-2.

Link 1D-2.
http://www.washingtonpost.com/news/post-nation/wp/2014/12/12/death-of-tamir-rice-12-year-old-shot-by-cleveland-police-ruled-a-homicide/

A long list of police killings

In case anyone thinks that police brutality is something new in America, there is a long list of incidents of police killings and brutality going back to 1951 in various states of America. An article in *Wikipedia* titled "List of cases of police brutality in the United States."

See link 1E.

Link 1E

http://en.wikipedia.org/wiki/List_of_cases_of_police_brutality_in_the_United_States

Some people will object saying that there have been many cases of blacks assaulting and killing white people. Yes, there have been cases of blacks killing and assaulting whites, but this is no excuse for police brutality against anyone, especially minorities. This subject is controversial and statistics on minority crimes against whites are hard to find, except for isolated cases.

The Case of Dillon Taylor

Steve Straub of *The Federalist Papers* reports on the killing of Dillon Taylor, 20 who was killed by a black policeman on August 11, 2014. The article is titled " Unarmed White Man Killed by Black Cop; Here's How the Media Reacted". A video by KUTV in Utah was included in the article. See link 1F.

Link 1F
http://www.thefederalistpapers.org/us/unarmed-white-man-killed-by-black-cop-heres-how-the-media-reacted

Dillon Taylor had committed no violent crime and was un-armed. But he was gunned down as if his name was Dillinger instead of Taylor!

Why were there no mass demonstrations against police brutality in the Dillon Taylor case? Is it just a routine police action when an un-armed white man is gunned down by a black policeman? No it is not routine! It is still police brutality regardless of the races involved on either side! And the American people should be disturbed by all such police violence in the case of non-violent crimes and un-armed individuals!

The case of George Hunley

Mr. Hunley was shot twice by criminals in an ambush when he stopped to help what he thought was a stranded car alongside the road. He reported the crime to police. When Mr. Hunley came home from the hospital he found the police searching his home and they would not let him enter his home. This was apparently a search without the presentation of a warrant beforehand to Mr. Hunley. This is apparently a case of abuse of police powers. The case occurred in the "enlightened" state of Virginia. The report was titled, Good Samaritan shot twice in Louisa: Deputies 'Treating me like a criminal'

Posted: Feb 05, 2015 2:02 PM CST
Updated: Feb 06, 2015 5:28 AM CST
By Ray Daudani,
Updated by Chris Thomas

See link 2F.

Link 2F.
http://www.waff.com/story/28036107/good-samaritan-shot-twice-in-louisa-deputies-treating-me-like-a-criminal

See link 1G.

Link 1G:
http://nypost.com/2014/12/20/2-nypd-cops-shot-execution-style-in-brooklyn/

Police brutality against white people

There is also a history of police brutality against white people. The homeless seem to be one target of police brutality. An excellent article "Is Police Brutality Color-blind?" by Nat Parry in the *Consortiumnews,* of August 22nd, 2014, describes the problem of police brutality that cuts across racial lines. Here is a quote from the article:

"In one recent case that received some national attention, police shot and killed a homeless white man in Albuquerque, New Mexico, sparking a wave of demonstrations in the city. Police officers gunned down 38-year-old James Boyd on March 16 in the Sandia foothills following a

standoff and after he allegedly brandished a small knife, authorities said. But a helmet-camera video showed Boyd agreeing to walk down the mountain, gathering his things and taking a step toward officers just before they opened fire."

The conclusion that we can make from the above, if true, is that police brutality, and the illegal use of force by police, is spread across races, although minorities seem to bear the brunt of the police brutality.

See link 1H.

Link 1H:
https://consortiumnews.com/2014/08/22/is-police-brutality-color-blind/

Are police killings necessary?

Are these killings really all necessary, or is it partly due to inadequate police training or weapons that are designed to kill instead of temporarily incapacitate? (Please note that I am not an advocate of extreme "gun control" laws.) I advocate research and development of practical non-lethal weapons that the police can use to subdue unruly persons for arrest, instead of resorting to dangerous, or potentially lethal tactics, or lethal weapons such as guns. If you can quickly incapacitate a culprit and arrest him or her alive, isn't that better than killing with a lethal weapon? Are guns the only thing we can resort to in the 21st Century? What about the Taser (TM) or some kind of non-lethal gas or spray? I used to be that police did just fine in controlling "bad guys" with just a club!

I am not saying police should not be armed with a lethal weapon, but I am saying that they need an alternate non-lethal weapon that they can use, especially if a culprit is not armed.

Is there a police culture that seeks to kill or seriously injure perceived criminals?

Is there a culture in some police departments that the crime situation has to be dealt with in whatever way is necessary to eliminate the criminals? *Kill them before they kill us*! Or have they a very tough attitude, and they will routinely apply heavy handed force, or even lethal force, on whoever they think fits their profile of a drug dealer or other heinous or violent criminal? I hope that is not the case, but there seems to be indications that such attitudes prevail in some jurisdictions. And if this is true, the bad attitude might eventually spread to all jurisdictions all over the country creating a virtual police state! I hope that this attitude problem can be corrected before it is too late.

Some jurisdictions will have reasonable police forces with good performance. Other jurisdictions will have tough police with questionable tactics and a lot of "incidents" that will alienate people's respect for the police, and that in turn will only aggravate the police problems *and the need for more police*!

Where does a bad police attitude originate?

Maybe some jurisdictions of police in America have such an attitude, but if they do, it may be not the idea of the policeman on the beat, or the lieutenant, or the captain, or even the chief of the police! It is more than likely the orders or direction of the top people in the jurisdiction like the mayor or councilmen.
Yes, problems always start at the top!

Are the police really at fault?

But in this book I do not intend to criticize the police. In fact all of the policemen I have ever met in the USA have always been professional and cordial to me. Of course, most likely I *do not* fit the profile of a heinous criminal either!
In defense of the police, they are under-staffed for the amount of crime in the country, they work on inadequate budgets, they are out-gunned by the criminals, and they are criticized at every turn, while they work under extreme pressures, and face extreme dangers. Extreme danger can create extreme fear, and extreme fear can cause

extreme responses, regardless of any other factors in anyone's experience, unless the police are highly qualified and extremely well trained to respond in a way that is correct and appropriate for the circumstance.

Should laws be changed?

Without changes in the laws of the USA or the way people are treated, crime will continue to increase in the USA, and the need for more and more police will continue to add to the police state powers in USA.
As lawmakers add more and more silly laws and continue the "war on drugs", the crime problem will only increase and even normally law abiding citizens will be caught in the police-judicial web system as "criminals".

Should a policy of gun control be put in force?

There are plenty of gun control laws already in effect. It is more important to enforce existing gun laws instead of creating new laws.
Known criminals, felons, and mentally ill persons should not be allowed to purchase guns by existing laws. But somehow criminals manage to obtain guns, and if law-abiding citizens cannot own guns they will be totally at the mercy of criminals.

A law abiding citizen should have the right to own guns for self protection in accordance with the second amendment to the U.S. Constitution.

> **The Second Amendment** of the United States Constitution reads: "A well regulated Militia, being necessary to the security of a free State, the right of the people to keep and bear Arms, shall not be infringed."

Killings of policemen

The ambush of two policemen in New York City

On December 20th of 2014, two NYPD policemen, Rafael Ramos and Wenjian Liu, were shot to death by a mentally deranged black man who had earlier in the day shot his girlfriend in the stomach. The incident was reported in the *New York Post* in an article titled "Gunman executes 2 NYPD cops in Garner 'revenge' " by Larry Celona, Shawn Cohen, Jamie Schram, Amber Jamieson and Laura Italiano, December 20, 2014.

The killer Ismaaiyl Brinsley, 28, had addresses in Georgia, Maryland, and Brooklyn.
He had a record of many violent crimes but was not held in prison. This is a case where a violent mentally ill criminal, known to have stolen a gun earlier in his criminal career, was allowed to roam the streets free to do more violent crime, while other men spend time in prison for non-violent crimes!
This incident only served to make community relations between citizens and the police even more divisive. A side effect of the ambush killing was to make the police feel that the Mayor, Bill de Blasio, was at fault for not condemning the protests against the police in the earlier case of the Garner police killing.
Is the animosity between the NYPD and the Mayor's office a taste of things to come possibly when the police revolt against civilian authority and the police become the rulers of society forming a true police state? I hope not!

How many police are killed in the line of duty?

According to the *National Law Enforcement Officers Memorial Fund*, more than 20,000 police officers have been killed in the line of duty since 1791 in the United States. On average, one officer is killed in the United States every 58 hours.

Law enforcement is a dangerous and difficult job and we always need to keep that fact in mind when we criticize or otherwise judge the actions of individual officers in any situation. See link 1I.

Link 1I.
http://www.nleomf.org/facts/

Summary

There is a serious crime problem in the U.S. because of discrimination against people of color. People of color often cannot obtain good jobs and pay because of discrimination. Some of them turn to crime as a way to survive in a desperate situation. Discrimination is a serious problem in the U.S. and when police have a racist attitude it can lead to police brutality and even killings in a few cases. There may be a culture of police brutality against people of color in some jurisdictions, especially when their leadership advances an attitude of aggressiveness against certain cultural groups or people of color. But police are killed too by criminals in large numbers every year, and often the police are perceived as brutal, or accused of discrimination when they are only doing their duty in a dangerous job. Laws need to be changed to reduce the number of arrests for trivial offenses. More gun control laws are not the answer to the crime problem.

As crime has grown, the number and the power of police have also grown.

**Chapter 2
The Prison Problem**

The prison population in America

America, that is the United States of America, has the largest prison population of any country in the world although it is not by far the most populous nation!
Here are the three largest country prison populations according to the *ICPS The International Centre for Prison Studies* :

USA 2,228,424
China 1,701,344
Russia 624,500

See the link no. 2 for more data:

link no. 2
http://www.prisonstudies.org/sites/prisonstudies.org/files/resources/downloads/wppl_10.pdf

Now let's compare the above numbers against the population of each of the three countries with the following "real time" data as of 2014 from *Worldometers, Real Time World Statistics* :

USA 322,533,006
China 1,393,783,836
Russia 142,467,651

Without getting into too much detail on this, it is a simple matter to calculate the percentages of the prison populations to the total populations of each of the three countries. We have the approximate ratios as follows:

USA 0.69 %
China 0.12%
Russia 0.44%

So from the above facts, we can safely say that either USA has a lot more criminals than either China or Russia in relation to its population, or *there is something definitely wrong in the USA!* According to the American Progress organization, 60% of the prison population of America is people of color. In addition, one in three black men can be expected to go to prison at some time in their lives. As you study the facts concerning the arrests of people of color, it appears that a pattern of discrimination is applied to people of color who are more likely to be arrested than white people. Black neighborhoods are usually the target of the "war on drugs" where more people are arrested for drug offenses than in white neighborhoods. Black juveniles are more likely to be put into detention centers and from there into prison than white boys. See link 2-1.

Link 2-1.
https://www.americanprogress.org/issues/race/news/2012/03/13/11351/the-top-10-most-startling-facts-about-people-of-color-and-criminal-justice-in-the-united-states/

Abuse of prisoners in the USA

Some prisons in the USA have really bad conditions where prisoners are abused and treated like animals. There have been cases of sexual harassment and abuse in many prisons. Cases of alleged abuse in Alabama prisons have been documented in an article titled "Alabama's Trouble Prisons" posted in *The Huntsville Times*, December 28, 2014 by AL.com. I quote from the report:

"On Jan. 17, the Department of Justice issues a report describing grim conditions at the Julia Tutwiler Prison for Women. Among the abuses it tells of prison staff members [allegedly] raping and fondling inmates, and of officials failing to investigate inmate allegations or stifling them. "The women at Tutwiler universally fear for their safety", the report states."

See link 2A:
Link 2A.

http://www.al.com/investigates/2014/09/alabama_prisons_are_underfunde.html

Women in prison for murder

Yes, many of the women in prison are have been sentenced for murder, usually a case where a desperate woman being abused and beaten by her husband eventually kills him in self defense. But of course there is usually no proof of self defense so the court puts the women in prison. In other cases, the women really need care for mental illness, but instead they get prison sentences. See link 2B.

Link 2B.
http://www.purpleberets.org/pdf/bat_women_prison.pdf

Taxpayer's money wasted putting mentally ill people in prison

In the USA there are many cases where a person may have committed a crime because of mental illness, but instead of getting proper psychiatric treatment, the individual is put in prison which will not help the individual get well and the taxpayer's money would be better spent in treating the mental illness problem! Over 700,000 mentally ill people were in US prisons in 2005. See link 2C.

Link 2C:
http://nicic.gov/mentalillness

Why are there so many people put in prison for minor infringements?

People are arrested for minor violations of the law and then judges sentence them to jail terms rather than make them do restitution or do public service.

As an example, the New York City Police Department has a policy called "Broken Windows". Basically this means that if police see broken windows in a neighbor hood and the windows are not repaired, the police will assume the neighborhood has "gangs" or "bad guys" and they will patrol it more often and make more arrests in that neighborhood than others that "look good", that is no broken windows that are not repaired. Of course this practice targets neighborhoods that have people who are poor and at the lower levels of income. Unfortunately, these people are also usually people of color due to the prevalence of discrimination and poor education in such neighborhoods.

The theory is that if people are arrested for petty crimes that will prevent them from doing worse crimes in the future, or if the neighborhood is more heavily patrolled there will be less crime. I might subscribe with and agree to the second part of the theory.

The policy appears to have reduced crime in NYC but there is no proof that the broken windows policy is the remedy for crime.

The main danger of such a policy is that it will tend to result in more arrests of people of color and possible lethal encounters that will enrage the community against the police.

I do believe that it is good to arrest people for minor crimes so that criminals do not just run amuck, but I don't think that jail terms are always appropriate. Again, I believe that restitution, or community services are better answers than jail whenever possible.

In the case of possessing small quantities of illegal drugs, again I think that a mandatory treatment and rehabilitation program is better than jail and would be a better way to spend taxpayer's money!

The so-called "war on drugs" needs to be curtailed, at least as far as minor drug possession and use is concerned.

Rick Hampson, of *USA Today* wrote an article titled "Voices: In New York, a debate over how to fight crime", dated January 22nd, 2015. See link 2D.

Link 2D.
http://www.usatoday.com/story/news/2015/01/22/bratton-policing-garner-new-york-city/22125315/

Example of punishment of a man convicted of drug possession

In 2003, Kyle Beebe, son of Arkansas Governor Beebe, was convicted of felony possession of marijuana. He has been in jail for 11 years for possession of a substance that is now legal in some states such as Colorado! Kyle is scheduled to be released in December of 2014 with a pardon from the Governor, his father, according to *USA Today*, "State-by-State News" of Friday, November 28, 2014.

Possession of marijuana in Arkansas can be a class A felony

Possession of 100 pounds or more in Arkansas is a class A felony and punishable for a prison term of from 6 to 30 years and a fine of $15,000. At link no. 15 you can read the complex and formidable laws on marijuana in Arkansas. The law is as tough for a non-violent crime such as possession of marijuana, as it is in some states for manslaughter or even murder!

link no. 15
http://www.criminaldefenselawyer.com/marijuana-laws-and-penalties/arkansas.htm

Second degree murder punishment in Arkansas is comparable to punishment for marijuana possession?

It is interesting to note that in Arkansas, the penalty for second degree murder is 6 to 30 years. This is the same as the penalty for the class A felony possession of marijuana, except that there is no monetary fine like the $15,000 fine for the marijuana possession! Apparently the State of Arkansas puts less value on the life of a person than on possession of 100 pounds of marijuana! The case of Kyle Beebe is a typical case of imprisonment of a person who has not committed a violent crime but has been caught in the web of criminal activity brought on bye the illegality of common drugs and the "war on drugs".
By the way I am not a marijuana user nor do I advocate the use of marijuana or any other addictive substance, except as prescribed by a doctor for the treatment of a medical condition. But I do believe that most drugs that are now illegal such as marijuana, cocaine, and methamphetamine, should be legalized (like alcohol and tobacco) to remove the black market and stop the drug criminal trafficking as I describe in more detail below.

The punishment for murder in America is different from state-to-state

For comparison to the Arkansas punishment for the possession of marijuana crime, link no. 16 provides a summary of the punishments for murder in each state of the United States. You will note a large degree of variation in punishments for murder in the United States from state- to- state. It is true that states have all powers not granted to the federal government according to the U.S. Constitution, but it is sad that a uniform code of punishment cannot be adopted in all states of the U.S.

link no. 16
http://en.wikipedia.org/wiki/List_of_punishments_for_murder_in_the_United_States

Imprisonment of thousands for non-violent crimes

I have written the above in this chapter to highlight the main problem with the justice system that has imprisoned hundreds of thousands of people for non-violent crimes as well as violent criminals. Unfortunately, the poor that are imprisoned do not have money to make bail, while the "big time" criminals can usually make bail and get their freedom quickly. Also such criminals can afford the best lawyers to get themselves acquitted in court, while the poor cannot and are convicted, sometimes for long sentences.

The poor man who is charged with a crime is more likely to get convicted by ambitious prosecutors who are trying to build their reputations as having good conviction records and judges who are anxious to "make examples" of people who have been caught doing certain crimes even the non-violent kind.

Violent criminals get back on the streets with "parole"

Even worse is the fact that violent criminals in many states are "paroled" without serving their full sentences. Many are again convicted of another violent crime and return to prison while others commit more violent crimes and are not apprehended. Why do we let violent criminals go back on the streets to commit more violent crimes while the jails are full of non-violent criminals?
Is it because of the liberal "do-gooders" that approve the parole of seasoned violent criminals, because they think that a violent person can be rehabilitated just because he has been in prison for a length of time?

What is the rate of recidivism after release from prison?

Fig. 3 shows the rate of recidivism by type of crime for prisoners released from prison from the

Bureau of Justice Statistics of the U.S. government. Refer to link no. 17 for the full report.

link no. 17
http://www.bjs.gov/content/reentry/recidivism.cfm

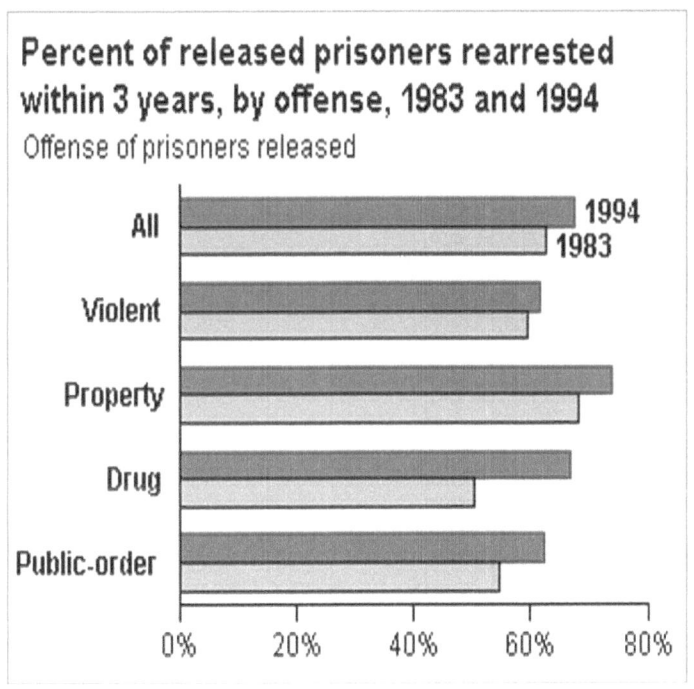

Fig. 3, Recidivism of U.S. Prisoners in 1983 and 1994, source *Bureau of Justice Statistics*, U.S. Government

From Fig. 3 we see that the recidivism rate is approximately 60% for violent criminals in 1983 and 1994 and showed no improvement over the 10 year period. Why then are violent criminals let out to do more mayhem on the streets? Also how many of the 40% who do not come back do violent crimes but are not caught or apprehended so they are not counted in the recidivism rate?

A major factor driving the need for more police

Recidivism is a major factor driving the need for an increased number of police and further development of the police state. This problem will only get worse with increasing population and the attendant increase in prison population if the judicial system and laws are not changed.

The growth in numbers and size of prisons

The growth in the number and size of prisons also increases the growth and size of the judiciary and the police required to support the prison system-- another factor in development of the police state!

Imprisonment does not help drug offenders

Also why are drug offenders put in jail and then released and over 65% go back to their drug way of life? What is the value of putting drug offenders in prison if their punishment is of almost no effect? In some states the sheriffs actually get paid a per diem for each prisoner they keep in jail so the more people they can arrest and put in jail on drug offenses like marijuana use or possession, the more money they make! Of course the taxpayers are footing the bill for this form of corruption!

Is taxpayer money being spent wisely on imprisoning drug addicts?

We are spending a lot of taxpayer money incarcerating drug addicts when the money would be better spent helping addicts to break the drug habit, and educating people about the dangers of drugs and the consequences of drug addition on health and well-being.

Why do we put property offenders in jail?

We can ask the same question about property offenders. In 1994, property offenders had a recidivism rate of approximately 75%.
Why were they put in prison in the first place? Would it not have been better to make these people do community service and work to make

restitution for their crime, instead of crowding the jails at taxpayer's expense while violent criminals are released to do more violent crimes such as assault, rape, and robbery with a deadly weapon?

Imprisonment for disorderly conduct?

Finally why put a person in prison for some type of disorderly conduct (Public-order crime?) Most likely such people need help such as counseling, or rehabilitation, for example if their behavior was alcohol induced, should they not be in a program to correct their alcohol problem instead of being imprisoned?

Prisons filled with non-violent criminals

The prisons in America are full of people who should not be there while people who should be there due to serious violent crime are let out on "parole" and likely to commit more violent crime!

Should violent criminals get parole?

If a person has committed a serious violent crime such as rape, murder, or armed robbery, can you ever really trust such a person to "go straight" no

matter how good a prisoner they have been while in prison?
Yes there may be mitigating circumstances such as bad health or old age that could be a reason to parole or release someone from prison, but other than those reasons, I don't see any justification that is possible to let a violent prisoner back on the streets.

If you have a "record" of imprisonment can you find a job?

Finally, the people who are put in prison for minor non-violent crimes, will find it difficult to find another job. This fact can cause a person to give up looking for legal work and decide to do illegal work, or in short, to become a real criminal!

"White collar" crimes

Some crimes, especially the so-called "white collar crimes" are open to question. For example, a stock broker or stock trader can be put in prison for using so-called "insider information" to make stock trades. But isn't the need for information the bread and butter of stock trading? Would you buy a stock if you did not know anything about it? What does it mater where the information comes from? If you get information that is considered "insider information", the chances are that other people have the same information. Should you sit on the sidelines and do nothing while others, who have the information also, reap large profits?

The case of Martha Stewart

Consider the case of Martha Stewart. She had to go to prison for 5 months followed by 5 months of house arrest and two years probation for supposedly using "inside information" to sell a stock she owned. From *Biography, Your Dictionary*, and the article "Why did Martha Stewart go to jail?" you can read the story. See link no. 18.

link no. 18
http://biography.yourdictionary.com/articles/why-did-martha-stewart-go-to-jail.html

Martha got information from her broker that a stock she owned was about to fail getting FDA approval for a drug that the company was working on. She got the information before the general public did. So was she supposed to just sit on the information knowing that she would take a big loss when the news became public? Or since she was the owner could she not sell the stock anytime she wanted to?

My opinion is that this was a marginal or even controversial action, as far as whether or not it violated any law that she took to protect her financial positions, and that it was no one's business what she did with the stock she owned.

Taxpayer money is wasted imprisoning non-violent criminals

In either case, what good did it do to send Martha Stewart to prison, and then keep her in house arrest and on probation, other than to waste taxpayer's money with the judicial proceedings, incarceration, and probation? Was it to make her an example? If that was the case, it did not work because there have been many such cases of similar nature that have followed her arrest!

What is the logic for putting non-violent criminals in prison?

There is no reason to put criminals in prison unless they pose a danger to society, either by violent criminal acts, or by acts that threaten the life, freedom, or personal finances of people and society if they are left at large.

A person who has committed violence against another, except in self defense, or is a known threat to society by his or her actions, cannot be trusted to be left free and should be incarcerated or institutionalized until he or she is no longer a danger to society.

In the case of non-violent criminals, taxpayer money is better spent rehabilitating someone who can be rehabilitated than spending money on prison incarceration.

Putting someone in prison should not be about punishment, revenge, or satisfying victims. It should only be used to protect society at large and in conformance with the US Constitution and all of the rights therein.

As for non-violent crimes that have done harm to someone's property or financial condition, but do not threaten anyone else or society at large, it is a lot better to require restitution to the victims than to incarcerate the criminal which virtually guarantees that there will be no restitution by the criminal.

Drug users are not really criminals unless they have committed a criminal act other than just using drugs. So there is no reason to incarcerate such individuals. Taxpayer money would be better spent on helping such people to be rehabilitated!

Prison Over-Crowding

One of the effects of our present judicial system and laws with the heavy handed arrests and convictions for even minor offenses is over-crowding of prisons.

According to the *Huffington Post* article by Kathleen Miles, titled "Just How Much The War On Drugs Impacts Our Overcrowded Prisons, In

One Chart", posted March 10, 2014, see link no. 19,

link no. 19
http://www.huffingtonpost.com/2014/03/10/war-on-drugs-prisons-infographic_n_4914884.html

Over 50% of prisoners are in for drug offenses. For most of them the "drug of choice" was marijuana!

The high cost of maintaining prisons

The following link from the *American Legislative Exchange Council* gives statistics on the prison system in the state of Texas. This state has a prison budget of over $3 billion annually to cover the cost of 111 prisons and taking care of inmates. There are over 150,000 prisoners incarcerated in the state of Texas and the average cost per inmate is over $18,500. Some honest people on the outside of prison don't even make that much money from their jobs! See link no. 20.

link no. 20
http://www.alec.org/initiatives/prison-overcrowding/prison-overcrowding-texas/

As a positive measure, the state of Texas is looking at doing rehabilitation of drug offenders instead of incarceration.

Prison Over-Crowding Solutions

There is an organization that proposes solutions to the excessive incarceration of Americans and the resulting over-crowding of prisons. It is the *American Legislative Exchange Council*. See link no. 21.

link no. 21
http://www.alec.org/initiatives/prison-overcrowding/

Criminal law needs an over-haul

However, I think that the real solution is a complete overhaul of criminal law and penalties to remove laws against crimes that are really only common cultural characteristics of our society, for example drug use and addiction, or behavioral "crimes" that come under the heading of "public order", some types of "white collar" crime, such as insider information on stock transactions, and many other so-called "crimes" that are really not deserving of imprisonment as punishment.

Treatment or punishment?

In many cases, an individual has committed some action that really requires mental evaluation and treatment, not imprisonment, unless the action is violent and causes harm to others.

The only real good reason for imprisonment of people

Violent crime, terrorism, and financial threats to society at large, where harm or potential harm to others is involved should be the only causes for imprisonment.

Better ways of handling cases of non-violent criminals

Non-violent crimes should be handled with measures outlined in the above link from the *American Legislative Exchange Council*. Measures such as fines, garnishment of wages, restitution, community service, military service, counseling, class studies, and electronically monitored limitations on movements, are better ways of treating non-violent criminals.
For example, in the state of Alabama, certain driving violations require that the driver not only pay a fine, but also attend "driver's education" classes conducted by the state or local jurisdiction.

Counseling and rehabilitation

There could also be required class room counseling sessions for drug possession and addiction, instead of imprisonment. Of course, as the drug laws stand right now, drug dealing is a serious crime and requires imprisonment to protect others from harm. We will discuss this problem more in a later chapter.

Prison can radicalize inmates

Preachers and representatives of various religions are allowed to come into U.S. prisons and proselytize prisoners with ideological sermons and lessons. It does not matter whether the instruction is Christian, Muslim, Jewish, or any other religion, theology, or ideology. Prisoners sometimes get radicalized. I believe that all religions should be banned from all U.S. prisons. The U.S. Constitution requires separation of church and state, and therefore prisons, being a function of the state, should ban all such groups from entering the prisons, and teaching religion or possibly even radical ideas to prisoners.
If some religious group was allowed to come into a public school and teach Christianity, for example, there would certainly be a lawsuit against that activity. So it is the same thing when a religious group enters a prison.

Of course there is always the danger that a prisoner will be radicalized in prison even if there is no religious group influencing the prisoner. This is a reason for minimizing the prison population to contain only violent people or people who are a risk to society in a major way. Another problem is that putting a man in prison is very likely to alienate that man against society. So if that man is subsequently released on parole or when he finishes his sentence and is released, there is a high probability that he will return to a life of crime and a danger that the man will become an even more dangerous violent criminal capable of heinous crimes. Therefore the goal should be to try to keep people out of prison for non-violent crimes and only incarcerate the criminals known to be violent.

Summary

America has more people in prison than any other country in the world. People are arrested for minor infractions and put in prison even though they are not violent. Many that are in prison are actually mentally ill and need treatment instead of incarceration which will not help them. The majority of violations are drug related cases with long prison sentences just for the possession of drugs. Prisoners after release have a very high recidivism rate so the prisons remain full and over-crowded. When a person has a prison record it is almost impossible to get a job so they return to their old ways and are eventually re-arrested and put back in prison. Too many people are in prisons for non-violent crimes costing tax payers huge amounts of money to support the prison population, guards, officials, and the infrastructure. Women are abused and miss-treated in prisons especially in southern states such as Alabama. Laws need to be changed to reduce the number of arrests and incarceration, especially for non-violent offenders who should be working to make restitution instead of wasting their time and taxpayer money in prison.

Chapter 3
The Justice System

The judicial problems

Justice is complex and different from one jurisdiction to another

The United States individual state and local judicial systems are different from one jurisdiction to the next. A violent criminal who has committed first degree murder can be sentenced to death in one state, but in another state the maximum sentence is life.

Eighteen states currently do not have a death penalty while the rest do for first degree murder. Lesser crimes are also treated differently in different jurisdictions. For example, a crime of stealing an automobile is a felony in most states, but the laws are different in each and every state for this crime. Link no. 12 lists the details of the laws regarding auto theft in each state.

link no. 12
http://www.criminaldefenselawyer.com/crime-penalties/federal/Grand-theft-auto.htm

What is the main problem with American justice?

But what is the main problem with the judicial system in any state that a crime is committed? It is referred to as the "revolving door" of criminal justice. In other words, a person who commits a crime such as burglary can be arrested, and then released from jail in the next day on bail or sometimes just released "on his own recognizance", only to go back on his burglary routine.

Habeas corpus

How does this happen? Usually a lawyer for the accused will submit a request for habeas corpus to have the prisoner appear before a judge. The judge will usually order the prisoner released pending trial or in the case of lack of sufficient evidence he may be permanently released. Or bail will be set. If the prisoner has backing or sufficient funds available, he or she can "make bail" and be released in a day or two. If the prisoner cannot produce the bail money from someone, he will remain in jail. In this way the jails become filled with the poor who do not have financial backing, while the criminals who are backed financially by someone will be released. In addition the criminals who are part of organized crime who get bailed out quickly, are usually the worst criminals.

Link no. 13 gives a good description of the process.

link no. 13
http://legal-dictionary.thefreedictionary.com/writ+of+habeas+corpus

How many criminals are actually detained following arrest?

A report titled "Criminal Justice Indicator Report, January 2013" from the office of the mayor, Michael R. Bloomberg and John Feinblatt, details the judicial process in the New York City area. See link no. 14 for the complete report.

link no. 14
http://www.nyc.gov/html/om/pdf/2013/criminal_justice_indicator_report_0113.pdf

You can deduce from the following chart from the report that many people arrested for felonies are released at arraignment, Fig. 1:

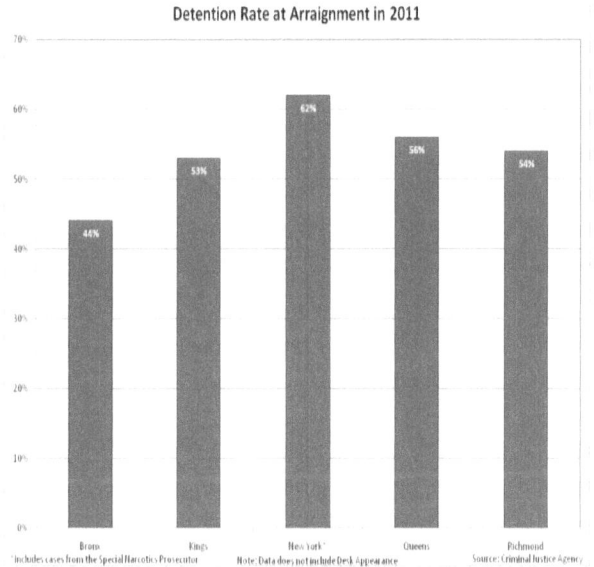

Fig. 1, Detention Rates in New York City Area

People committing felonies are released back onto the streets

The average detention rate for felonies is approximately 54% according to the report. Therefore, approximately 46%, almost half, of the people arrested on a felony charge are not detained! In other words, someone who is arrested under suspicion of committing rape, has a 46% chance of being released back onto the streets in New York City!

We see the need for more police to be on the streets because of the inefficiency of the justice system that results in even more crimes by violent criminals who should have been kept in jail instead of released on bond or some legal technicality.

On the other hand some "criminals" are unfairly handed long sentences "to make an example of them" by a judge who has some ax to grind.

The Capricious Nature of Justice in the United States

Link no. 22 provides a summary of the punishments for murder in each state of the United States. You will note a large degree of variation in punishments for murder in the United States.

link no. 22

http://en.wikipedia.org/wiki/List_of_punishments_for_murder_in_the_United_States

Link no. 23 provides a list of states that have the death penalty for murder and the ones that do not.

link no. 23
http://www.deathpenaltyinfo.org/states-and-without-death-penalty

In the footnotes on the list of states that have eliminated the death penalty, you will note that the following states have passed laws eliminating the death penalty but they did not make the death penalty retroactive so there are still prisoners sitting on death row awaiting their uncertain fate!

Connecticut 2012, 11 people still on death row.
Maryland, 2013, 5 people still on death row.
New Mexico 2009, 2 people still on death row.

Why are these people still on death row, when the death penalty has been abolished? Are these states still going through with executions in their cases? What kind of "uniform justice" is that? Also, if they are still to receive the death penalty even though the death penalty has been abolished, it is then cruel and unusual punishment, and against the U.S. Constitution.

Is the death penalty cruel and unusual punishment?

Here I should note that I am neither for nor against the death penalty. But I am for uniform justice throughout the land, against capricious justice, and un-fair justice in the justice systems of the United States!

An argument could be made that life sentences are cruel and unusual punishment and that a swift death penalty is the correct punishment in capital murder cases.

It could also be argued that keeping someone in prison for life is a very costly form of punishment and is a burden on the taxpayer!

On the other hand paroling someone who committed a violent, but non-lethal, crime is a risk to society when that violent person is released. Maybe the criminal has been reformed and maybe he or she has not. There is no foolproof way to know.

Is there a way to make punishment for crimes uniform under a judicial code decided on by the Supreme Court and the Congress, or should the punishment for each and every crime be decided by a judge that might be under the control of some politician, or a judge that is incompetent and has no qualifications to be a judge?

The U.S. Constitution grants all powers to the states that are not specifically granted to the Federal Government. So it is unlikely that there will ever be a uniform code of justice for all jurisdictions. However, the Federal Government could issue a suggested judicial code for the states to use, perhaps with incentives such as monetary aid for police and court systems when a state uses the code.

Strange sentences for non-violent crimes

Often judges give non-violent criminals, or even people who are really not criminals and have no criminal record, strange and cruel sentences just to make examples of them or even maybe just because they have some personal ax to grind. The following is an example from an article in *USA Today* titled "Driver who stopped for ducks gets jail, 10-year driving ban", by Melanie Eversley, December 19th, 2014.

In the article we read that Emma Czornobaj stopped for some ducklings that were crossing the Canadian highway she was driving on. A man and his daughter were riding behind Emma's car on a motorcycle and ran into the back of her car when she stopped. The man and his daughter were killed in the accident. Here I emphasize the word *accident*!

Emma was sentenced as being criminally negligent, causing death, and dangerous driving causing death. She was sentenced to 90 days in prison and a 10 year driving ban.

Now given that the case was in Canada, and even granting that she should not have made a sudden stop on a highway, should she have been put in prison for 90 days, and slapped with a 10 year driving ban, as if she was a criminal, or a drunken driver? No, a much lesser sentence, if any was in order for her action, I believe. I think this is a good example of justice gone wrong! See link 24.

Link 24.
http://www.usatoday.com/story/news/world/2014/12/17/canada-ducklings-highway-fatal-court/20513845/

If you think that strange courtroom sentences are rare, take a look at the blog *Off the Record*, in an article by Mark Harris, "**Judges Gone Wild! 14 Weird and Unusual Criminal Sentences**. See link 25.

Link no. 25.
http://www.crschools.net/blog/14-weird-and-unusual-criminal-sentences/

Are arrests for petty crimes really necessary?

There is one ray of hope in the judicial mess. As I am writing this, Seattle Washington is cutting back on arrests for petty crimes. For example, a homeless man charged with vagrancy, or urinating in public, may not do jail time.
The police and the justice system are overloaded with court cases for petty crimes while the real

criminals escape through the "cracks" and are released back on the streets.

The NYPD is also cutting back on tickets and arrests for petty crimes at the time I am writing this book, but they are doing this as a form of labor "strike", or as a way to the protest against the supposed wrongs of Mayor Bill de Blasio. Is this the start of the police powers starting to challenge civilian authority?

The poor and mentally ill stay in jail

The poor criminals cannot pay bail so they just stay in jail, while the criminals with money or a family with money get bailed out. So the jails are full of the poor people, who are mostly non-violent.

Also the jails are crammed with people who have mental illness and need treatment instead of jail time which only adds to their problems.

In the case of the mentally ill, the taxpayer is paying to keep mentally ill people in jail which does them no good whatsoever, when instead it would be a greater benefit to the mentally ill and to society, if the money was spent to provide treatment for them. Some of them can be treated or put on medication to become people who can live normal lives.

The problem is described in an article in USA Today titled "Solutions to woes of mentally ill exist but aren't used" by Liz Szabo, printed December 26th, 2014. See link no. 26.

Link no. 26.
http://www.usatoday.com/story/news/nation/2014/12/22/solutions-mental-illness/18816843/

Should judges be appointed or elected?

Judges at the higher levels are appointed, usually by politicians. This practice is not a good one. Judges who are appointed by politicians may be under undue political influence. Any judge who is appointed in any manner is beholden to whoever appointed him or her.
Instead, all judges should be elected by the people of their district if they are judges in local jurisdictions. Also the terms should not exceed four years to avoid any particular judge to develop entrenched power with the police and prosecutor in his or her jurisdiction.

Federal judges

Judges on the federal level should also be elected by the people, not appointed by politicians or even by the Congress, except for Supreme Court judges who are appointed by the President and approved by Congress.

Federal judges at lower levels should be elected to serve only in the individual states and not in regions covering more than one state, to avoid conflicts with people of different states and their individual laws.

Should the power of judges be limited?

Judges should be more limited in what kinds of sentences they can impose by the state legislatures, or preferably according to a uniform national judicial code described above.
No judges should be allowed to hand down unusual sentences or unusual punishments in violation of the Eighth Amendment to the Constitution of the United States that limits cruel or unusual punishment, either at the federal or state levels. See link 27.

Link 27.
http://en.wikipedia.org/wiki/Eighth_Amendment_to_the_United_States_Constitution

But despite the fact of the Eighth Amendment, judges persist in handing down crazy, cruel, and biased decisions for personal reasons, or to "make an example of someone", or for political or other reasons that are not justified by the case.

Why does it take so long for a person charged with a crime to get a trial?

Judges and courts are overloaded with cases for petty crimes, for example drug possession. The "war on drugs" and other politically inspired laws cause the arrest and incarceration of many people who should not be arrested. See Fig. 4 and Link 28 and 28A.

Link 28.
http://www.bop.gov/about/statistics/statistics_inmate_offenses.jsp

What are the main reasons for incarceration?

The data in Fig. 4 is from link 28, above. You will note that the major reason for incarceration is for drug offenses at 48.7% of prisoners. Weapons, explosives, and arson are the next biggest categories, followed by immigration violations.
As we shall see in the next chapters, arrests for drug violations can be drastically reduced by changes in laws.
Immigration violations can be reduced by reducing the influx of illegal immigrants and by accepting more people through legal channels of immigration. See Chapter 7.

The following is from link 28:

Chart Label	Offense	# of Inmates	% of Inmates
a	Banking and Insurance, Counterfeit, Embezzlement	730	0.4%
b	Burglary, Larceny, Property Offenses	7,899	4.0%
c	Continuing Criminal Enterprise	456	0.2%
d	Courts or Corrections	810	0.4%
e	Drug Offenses	97,252	48.7%
f	Extortion, Fraud, Bribery	12,345	6.2%
g	Homicide, Aggravated Assault, and Kidnapping Offenses	5,746	2.9%
h	Immigration	20,137	10.1%
i	Miscellaneous	1,547	0.8%
j	National	76	0.0%

k	Security Robbery	7,403	3.7%
l	Sex Offenses	13,501	6.8%
m	Weapons, Explosives, Arson	31,925	16.0%

Statistics based on prior month's data -- -- Last Updated: Saturday, 29 November 2014
Please Note: Data is limited due to the availability of offense-specific information.

Fig. 4, Criminal Offenses of the Imprisoned

Most crimes are "victimless" crimes

Link 28A states that 86% of crimes are "victimless" in the federal prison populations. They are including drug offenses and public order crimes which add to 85.7%. My question is why are public order offenses even in federal prisons in the first place?

I do not fully trust the statistics of link 28A, but it is clear that there are a lot of people in federal prisons that do not belong there!

Link 28A.
https://www.libertariannews.org/2011/09/29/victimless-crime-constitutes-86-of-the-american-prison-population/

We need a judicial "watch-dog"!

Each state legislature should have a "watch-dog" committee that periodically reviews the performance and decisions of each judge in his or her jurisdiction, and has the power to relieve any judge for cause by a majority vote of the legislature, and call for new elections to elect a new judge.
A similar "watch-dog" committee in the US Congress should have similar powers to recall federal judges as required to maintain order, efficiency, and good performance in the federal judicial system.

The Grand Jury System, Good or Bad, and how does it work?

The grand jury system in the USA is designed to give people the power to indicate that a crime has probably been committed, or not, and to indict, or not indict, the suspect for *probable cause* of committing a crime.

Why are grand jury deliberations kept secret?

The results of a grand jury deliberation are kept secret so witnesses are protected and can speak freely without fear of retaliation. Even high level persons such as politicians or other officials can be indicted by a grand jury.

What powers does a grand jury have?

A grand jury can force witnesses to testify and can require that any evidence available be presented to it for deliberation. A grand jury can decide that a crime has or has not been committed and can indict a person or persons that are involved in the criminal activity.

Who is in charge of the grand jury?

There is no judge present, but the grand jury system is under the tutelage of a prosecutor. The prosecutor can still prosecute a criminal even if the grand jury does not indict the suspect. However, usually the prosecutor will use the results of the grand jury deliberations to decide whether to prosecute or not. If no indictment is returned by the grand jury, it is not likely that the prosecutor will proceed with a court trial.

How does the grand jury come to a decision on a case?

The decision of a grand jury to prosecute does not have to be unanimous but a majority of usually 2/3 or 3/4 is normally used to decide if an indictment is to be issued, depending on the state where the grand jury is deliberating.

What are the advantages and disadvantages of the grand jury system?

The grand jury system is a good system in that it allows for protection of witnesses and has the ability to indict even high officials for crimes. It does however have the disadvantage of being under the tutelage of the prosecutor who might be biased and attempt to influence the grand jury accordingly.

How often are police officers indicted for crimes?

It is interesting to note that police officers are almost never indicted for crimes. This may be due to the fact that the prosecutor's office is usually closely aligned with police departments and therefore has a bias in favor of the police.

Do all states in USA have the grand jury system?

All states in USA can use the grand jury system but not all do so. Some states use a process called *a preliminary hearing.* The preliminary hearing is done under a judge and is not secret, so the preliminary hearing process is an inferior short cut method and subject to bias and abuse by a prosecutor or judge.

How could the grand jury process be improved?

A better way to manage a grand jury other than the by the local prosecutor, would be to have an elected official in each jurisdiction, independent of the local police and the judiciary, but having the use of the courts and having judiciary powers as needed. This official should report only to the state legislature or the governor of the state to make him as independent as possible and not under the influence of the police or judges in the judiciary system.
Such a system would still be in conformance with the 5th Amendment to the U.S. Constitution.

How many people make up a grand jury?

A federal grand jury can include form 16 to 23 people. A state grand jury is usually 12 to 23 people, except in Virginia where a grand jury can be 5 to 7 persons.

The right to a grand jury is protected by the 5th Amendment to the Constitution of the United States.

For more information on the grand jury system, see link no. 29 and link no. 30.

Link 29.
http://criminal.findlaw.com/criminal-procedure/how-does-a-grand-jury-work.html

Link 30.
http://en.wikipedia.org/wiki/Grand_jury

State and Federal laws create larger police numbers, over-crowded court rooms, and prisons

State and federal lawmakers have created a byzantine structure of complex and crazy laws that cause too many actions of individuals and corporations to be "crimes", overloading the justice system with arrests for trivial cases.

But the police, prosecutors, judges, and prisons love the system! Why? Because all of the trivial crimes are easy to deal with and guarantee easy jobs for police, prosecutors, judges, and the power of sheriffs and prison wardens with the increase of the number and size of prisons, especially the privately owned prisons-for-profit systems.

Summary

Forget about the "military-industrial complex". The military has been gutted and our industrial system is old and decrepit. *The new threat is the police-justice-prison complex!*

State and federal laws are out of control and cause an excessive number of activities to be classified as crimes, requiring large numbers of police, courts, judges, and prisons with large numbers of prisoners.

Examples: The "war on drugs", "insider trading", urinating in public, drunkenness (except DUI), spitting in the gutter, vagrancy, possession of marijuana, some traffic violations, some parking tickets, speed traps, prostitution, illegal immigration, etc.

Prosecutors are not impartial but are often allied with police to get convictions, even if a person is really innocent of a crime.

Prisons are over-crowded and in some cases sheriffs get paid a per diem for each prisoner they can keep in jail, giving them an incentive to arrest and jail as many people as they can, no matter how trivial the offense is.

Non-violent or mentally ill criminals and drug offenders, are put in prison instead of doing community service or getting treatment for their mental illness or addiction.

The U.S. justice system does not follow a uniform code from one jurisdiction to another. Judges decisions are often cruel and unusual violating the U.S. Constitution that bans "cruel and unusual punishment". Judges have too much power and do not answer to the people. Judges are appointed by politicians in many cases and can be under the influence of their political leaders to the detriment of fair justice, especially in cases where individuals have support, financial or otherwise, from politicians. Grand juries are often influenced by prosecutors who may be allied with the police.

Chapter 4
The War on Drugs and how to stop it

Illegal Drugs

Drug use and distribution is out of control

The illegal use and distribution of drugs and narcotics in the USA is out of control. The drug problem is a multifaceted problem. Here are just some to the reasons the drug trade is so large in the country:

The lure of drug dealing vs. getting a job

a) The shortage of good paying jobs is one of the causes for young men to start dealing drugs to bring in an income. The lack of jobs for young men, especially men without an education, creates a situation where it is easier and more profitable to deal drugs than find a job. This is the main reason for the criminal drug operations resulting in crimes of various types such as burglary, robbery, prostitution, and even murder. An aggravating factor is that the minimum wage requirement causes job qualifications to be tough. Usually even a menial job requires a high school diploma.

Drug use is related to poverty

b) People want drugs to escape from the terrible reality of the poverty they live in.

Young people are tempted by peer pressure

c) Young people use drugs to be "cool" at parties and to be accepted by their peers who are also using drugs.

Drugs are used in prostitution and illegal activities

d) Drugs are used by pimps to control prostitutes or women enslaved into prostitution.

Doctors prescribe "painkillers" and controlled substances

e) Unscrupulous doctors hand out prescriptions for pain killers and tranquilizers and other controlled substances without regard to the damage they are causing.

Do drug users commit crimes?

Does the drug user commit crimes? Maybe but in a most cases the drug user simply uses the drugs to escape the problems of the world or for recreational drug use as I mentioned above.

America leads the world in drug use

According to a report by Jennifer Warner of *CBS News*, titled "U.S. Leads the World in Illegal Drug Use", Americans are well ahead of all other countries in the illegal use of drugs, even the Netherlands which has very liberal drug laws! See link no. 7 for the complete story.

link no. 7
http://www.cbsnews.com/news/us-leads-the-world-in-illegal-drug-use/

The large usage of cocaine in America

According to the National Institute on Drug Abuse, there were about 1.9 million users of cocaine along in the U.S in 2008. The complete report is found at link no. 8.

link no. 8
http://www.drugabuse.gov/publications/research-reports/cocaine/what-scope-cocaine-use-in-united-states

The government's "war on drugs" is ineffective

Drug abuse and the drug dealing is certainly one of the main causes of crime in America. But here I would like to note that the drug related crime problem is analogous to the prohibition era in USA when crime was fueled by the demand for alcoholic drinks. Now crime is fueled by the demand for drugs under the prohibition of drug use by government laws and the so-called "war on drugs" which has not really solved the problem.

What is wrong with the "War on Drugs"?

First of all the so-called "War on Drugs" is based on the assumption that the government should prevent people from using drugs other than by doctor prescriptions. Accordingly, the government has passed laws making drug possession and drug dealing illegal.

In making these laws, the government has created a black market in drugs that opens the door for criminal activity by drug dealers who want to make the big money involved in supplying the black market.

What effect does the war on drugs have on police resources?

Then the government compounds the error by creating the "War on Drugs" which requires the huge resources of police, the FBI, and even the military attempting to stem the flow of drugs in the black market. This is another way the police powers have been expanded in the United States and other countries.

Has the "War on Drugs" been successful?

The fact is that the "War on Drugs" has not solved the problem. Drug dealing continues and drug king-pins make huge sums of money allowing them to corrupt public officials and police in the countries that supply drugs to USA and other countries.

The "War on Drugs" is like "prohibition" in USA

The situation in USA is much like the prohibition of alcoholic drink in the 1920's and early 1930's before the prohibition law was over-turned and alcohol became legal again. But during the "prohibition era" crime reached staggering proportions in the USA and many people were sickened by bad or contaminated alcohol. The prohibition era crime is very similar to the drug crime we have today in the drug black market

Illegal drug use in America has caused crime and violence in Mexico

The US consumption of illegal drugs has created the large illegal drug operations in Mexico which has caused violence in Mexico between rival drug dealers fighting each other for control of the illegal drug black market. The US "War on Drugs" was supposed to help Mexico suppress the illegal drug manufacturing operations and the drug dealers, but many people say that since the "War on Drugs" started in 2006, the drug dealers have only become more powerful and the level of violence has increased.

The only real solution is to eliminate the black market by making drugs legal and cheaply available, so there is no profit to produce them illegally. By eliminating the drug black market, the criminal drug dealers will suddenly be out of business if the previously illegal drugs are then made available under government control similar to the controls on alcohol and tobacco.

Why is alcoholic drink different than illegal drugs?

Alcoholic drink is a drug like any other that can affect mental capacity, be addictive, and affect health, even the legal varieties we have today. There is also the mental impairment effect that causes so many "drunk driving" deaths and injuries. So why is not alcohol also covered by the so-called "War on Drugs"? Obviously because alcoholic drink is now legal and controlled *and we have decided to accept the problems that go with it rather then going back to a "prohibition" or illegal status*!

Why is tobacco legal if it is just as damaging as illegal drugs?

The same is true of the drug nicotine that is legal to purchase in the form of tobacco and is under government control. The health effects of smoking such as cancer and emphysema are just as devastating as any of the now illegal drugs, or even worse. So, again why is tobacco not illegal? The use of tobacco parallels the use of marijuana except that the effects on health are different for marijuana.

What is wrong with the quality of illegal drugs?

Today, the black market illegal drugs are also contaminated or impure, and can cause a loss of mental capacity, sickness, and damaged health just like black market alcoholic drink that often contained the poisonous metal lead during the prohibition period.

Addiction and illegality sustains the black market

But people get addicted to the drugs and demand more and more, thus sustaining the black market. At the same time the government spends many millions fighting the war on drugs, it spends little on treatment for addicts, or on educational programs to teach people the dangers of drug use and addiction.

What is the solution to the crime problem associated with illegal drugs?

The obvious solution is to make the currently used illegal drugs legal! Whoa, you say we cannot do that! But we did it with alcohol drink and also the drug nicotine is legal in cigarettes, cigars, and the use of tobacco in pipes and chewing tobacco.
By making the drugs legal the government can gain control and even manufacture or control the manufacture of the drugs at a very low cost to the user so that the criminal element cannot make

money, and there will be no black market for criminals to supply to.

The government could control the manufacture and the purity of drugs

By controlling the manufacture and quality of drugs, the government can lower the toxicity of drugs and lessen the effects on the health of users. The government could also stay one step ahead of illegal drug makers by inventing new and better drugs that are less damaging to health but still provide the recreational quality for users.

The government could start a program of education and treatment for drug users

In order to reduce the demand for drugs, the government could now shift resources from police work to education and treatment programs for users to help users get off of the drugs and discourage the development of new drug users.

Drug offenses are the major cause of imprisonment

On September 30th of 2013, there were 98,200 prisoners in the US federal prison system serving time for drug offenses, or approximately 51% of the total federal prison inmates.
In the state prisons, there were 210,200 prisoners serving time for drug offenses or 16% of the state

prison population. Of the 16%, 25% were female and 15% were male.

Marijuana/hashish offenses were 12.4% of the drug offender population in federal prisons, and 12.7% in state prisons. So marijuana offenses are significant but not most of the drug offenses. See link 31.

States legalizing marijuana use for recreational purposes

Four states have made marijuana legal for recreational use: Alaska, Colorado, Oregon, and Washington. See link 32.

States legalizing marijuana for medical use

Twenty-three states and the District of Colombia (Washington DC) have made marijuana legal for medical use. See link 33.

Link 31.
http://www.drugwarfacts.org/cms/prisons_and_drugs#sthash.aJoz24oJ.dpbs

Link 32.
http://www.governing.com/gov-data/state-marijuana-laws-map-medical-recreational.html

Link 33.

http://medicalmarijuana.procon.org/view.resource.php?resourceID=000881

Continuing arrests and incarceration for marijuana offenses

But despite the legalization of marijuana in some states, other states continue to arrest and imprison people for possessing marijuana.
Here is an example of a petty arrest by police in the state of New Hampshire as reported in *USA Today* in the section "State-by-State" on January 15, 2015. Police seized 132 marijuana plants from a man's home and arrested him on a charge of allegedly "manufacturing a controlled substance". This is ridiculous. Is 132 plants really a "manufacturing" operation? I don't think so, and who cares if the man grows some marijuana for himself and his friends?
This is also an example of the non-uniformity of the justice system in the US where something that is legal in some states, is not legal in other states. So some people are put in jail while others enjoy doing the same thing freely!

Prostitution and drugs

Currently there are many women who are enslaved and exploited by "pimps" or slave-master criminals that hold woman essentially

captive, and make them dependent on drugs to do their bidding, prostituting themselves.
There are rumors of these women being beaten or even murdered if they do not do as they are told, or can no longer function as the slave-master wants
The pimps or slave-masters should be arrested and incarcerated for life as violent criminals and a danger to society.
But there will always be a demand for prostitutes unfortunately.

Should prostitution be legalized?

One solution to the problem of drug related prostitution, is to make prostitution legal and controlled by the local government with social services and health check-ups for their protection, and protection of the public from deadly venereal diseases such as HIV. Prostitutes will be required to register and be subject to periodic health examinations.
Also, if the prostitutes work out of a house or for an organization, the house or organization must be licensed, inspected, and regulated by the local government.
Under a program of the legalization of drugs, a prostitute can obtain her drugs at low cost and does not need to depend on a pimp or slave master for drugs. Also, social services can work with them to help them kick their habits and

possibly be rehabilitated back into society as productive citizens.

The dangers of drug use

Some people, especially young people, may think taking drugs will not hurt them. But there are many bad side effects, mental and physical problems. Below, I have listed the effects of the major drugs on health in order to show that the effects of drug use are very significant and dangerous.
This is one of the reasons that illegal drugs need to be brought under control, and legalizing illegal drugs is the only way to control their distribution and use. We have already learned this fact in the case of alcohol consumption under "prohibition". Why have we not learned the lesson relative to the illegal drugs?

Cocaine

There are many dangers to the use of cocaine. The following are some of the main health effects of using cocaine. See link 34 for additional information.

1. Heart attack or strokes.

2. Severe allergic reaction.

3. Changes to the brain cause addiction to the drug.

4. Injection can be a risk for HIV, hepatitis C, and other diseases.

5. Snorting can cause loss of smell, nose bleed, runny nose, and problems with swallowing.

6. Headaches.

7. Gastrointestinal tract complications, stomach pain, and nausea.

8. Elevated blood pressure and heart rate, leading to hypertension and possible stroke or heart attack.

9. Malnourishment due to loss of appetite.

10. Psychological effects such as anxiety, irritability, severe paranoia, and auditory hallucinations.

11. In combination with other drugs such as alcohol or heroin can lead to fatal overdose.

See link 34.

Link 34.
http://www.drugabuse.gov/publications/drugfacts/cocaine

Heroin

The main effects of heroin use are summarized here:

1. Changes in the physical structure of the brain.

2. Deterioration of the white matter of the brain.

3. Imbalances in bodily systems such as the hormonal system.

4. Increasing tolerance and addiction leading to the need to use more and more of the drug.

5. Withdrawal symptoms include pain, nausea, diarrhea, leg movements, cold sweats, etc. the withdrawal symptoms may last for months making it very difficult to break the habit.

6. Once a person is addicted, obtaining and using the drug becomes their main desire and they will do almost anything to get the drug.

7. As with cocaine, there is also the risk of getting serious diseases such as HIV by sharing needles with drug injection.

See link 35 for more information.

Link 35.
http://www.drugabuse.gov/publications/research-reports/heroin/what-are-long-term-effects-heroin-use

Meth-Amphetamine

1. Addiction and changes in the brain with development of tolerance requiring larger and larger doses for the pleasurable effect. As with other illegal drug addiction, the user's main desire becomes obtaining and using the drug.

2. The development of psychoses such as anxiety, confusion, insomnia, violent behavior, paranoia, hallucinations, and delusions.

3. Psychotic symptoms can last for months or years after cessation of the drug. Also stress can re-trigger the various psychoses listed in item 2 above.

4. Reduced motor speed in movements and mental impairment that can cause serious accidents while driving or operating machinery.

5. Impaired learning ability.

6. Functional changes in the brain that affect emotions and memory.

See link 36 for more information.

Link 36. http://www.drugabuse.gov/publications/research-reports/methamphetamine/what-are-long-term-effects-methamphetamine-abuse

Marijuana

There are many adverse health effects of using marijuana especially for young people. The following is a simplified list of some of these adverse health effects:

1. Increased risk of heart attack within hours of using the drug.

2. Mental illness.

3. Lung infections (the risk of cancer is unknown, but likely.)

4. Loss of IQ, especially in young users.

5. Memory loss, possibly permanent.

6. Impairment of judgment and motor coordination. Using the drug while driving, doubles the risk of being involved in an accident.

7. Development of psychoses, including suicidal thoughts in young users, depression, anxiety, personality disturbances, and a lack of motivation.

8. Damage to the brain of the fetus in pregnant users.

9. Addiction and drug craving after withdrawal.

See link 37 for more information on the health effects of the non-medical use of marijuana.

Link 37.
http://www.drugabuse.gov/publications/drugfacts/marijuana

Summary of the drug problem in the U.S.

The use and abuse of illegal drugs is a significant danger to the health of the users of drugs and creates a criminal empire to supply the black market. The "war on drugs" has resulted only in serving to increase the number and power of police in the U.S.
Without government control of the drugs the problem cannot be solved by the police. The drugs must be brought under the control of the

government by means of legalization, elimination of the black market (reducing prices of the drugs and making the drugs freely available), education of the public on the health dangers of the drugs, and creating treatment programs, instead of just arresting and imprisoning people for drug possession.

Chapter 5
Free Trade is not Fair Trade, and Foreign Aid drains the U.S. Treasury

One of the biggest do-gooder give-away programs costing Americans trillions in lost jobs and the loss of wealth of America has been accomplished by the liberal-progressive political establishment which has secretly sought to boost the welfare of other nations at the expense of America.
The far left liberal do-gooder people have done everything possible to reduce American wealth and power in the world, from "foreign aid" to "free trade" programs that work against small business and taxpayers.
I will show how the free trade programs have cost millions of American jobs resulting in increased crime and the expansion of police powers to fight the resulting increased crime. The liberal-progressives have even managed to convince conservatives that foreign aid and free trade is necessary, when all the foreign aid does is line the pockets of crooked politicians over-

seas, and free trade has virtually destroyed the industrial base of America.

The U.S. treasury has been plundered by the "foreign aid" program and the wealth of the country has been frittered away by the "free trade" programs so that the U.S. cannot even afford to repair its infrastructure, especially roads and bridges, not to speak of new infrastructure programs that are sorely needed, such as high speed rail and mass transit.

Not only have American jobs been lost due to "free trade" but also entire industries along with the associated skills, never to be recovered again for Americans.

America has lost job skills in all areas so now people cannot find jobs and some will turn to crime to survive.

America is about to descend into chaos unless policies change soon. As chaos ensues the police powers will expand at the expense of freedoms and America will become a dictatorship under the control of a police bureaucracy.

Free Trade

"Free trade" is a practice promoted by politicians of both parties to try to show that they are supporting business by expanding trade with other countries and that it is supposedly good for American businesses. A little analysis will show that "free trade" is really not good for the partners that have high labor rates. In most cases, American "free trade" with other less developed nations is really a give-away program and in a few cases has done America a lot of damage by building up the manufacturing base of potential future enemies.

But the important part relative to this book is that when America allows "free trade" with a lower labor rate country, the trade becomes one-sided and American businesses are wiped out because they cannot compete with the low labor rates of a third world or developing country.

Most foreign countries have a lower labor rate than America

The problem is that most other countries that America trades with have lower labor costs then do American businesses. So most products made in America are too expensive to be bought by countries like China, Korea, and other Asian countries (see the section above on the "minimum wage" problem.)

The only exceptions are certain high technology products made by America that are not yet available in other countries. Now if the trade was really free, there are certain un-named countries that would certainly like to buy our high technology products so they can copy and steal our technology for themselves.

How is all of this pertinent to this book? The so-called "free trade" is the main cause of the loss of many manufacturing jobs in America and has a direct relationship to the increase in crime when people cannot find jobs, because the jobs they could qualify for have gone overseas!

High technology trade restrictions

Fortunately, we usually have some restrictions so that the high technology products that would potentially be of military value are not allowed to be sold to foreign countries. But then it is not really a free trade program for America, is it? We can't really export much because our labor costs are too high in most products, and we can't export the high technology products. So our best and brightest businesses cannot really participate in the "free trade."

American food products are competitive

Now it is true that we can export food products such as wheat and corn on a competitive basis, but that is not a lot of help to our manufacturing companies and job creation.
On the other hand, many foreign countries are able to sell their products cheaply to America with big profits. For example, America has been flooded with cheap tools from China, and Americans the cheap tools instead of buying quality made American tools. Over the years with the so-called free trade program, America helped

China to set up a large manufacturing base that Americans have unwittingly paid for!

The U.S. trade deficit

What are the numbers? Let's look at the facts. In *MarketWatch*, reporter Jerry Bartash states:
"The U.S. trade deficit with China rose 2.7% in July to a record high $30.9 billion, a reflection of the changing fortunes in the two giant economies."
See link no. 6 for the complete story.

Link no. 6
http://www.marketwatch.com/story/us-trade-deficit-with-china-hits-record-high-2014-09-04

The relationship between "free trade" and the crime problem in America

Now how does free trade cause America to further build its police state? The answer is simple. So-called free trade actually hurts the manufacturing businesses in the USA causing lost jobs and fewer new jobs available for American workers. It also forces USA companies that are competing with foreign imports to keep their wages artificially low, or even move their operations to low-labor rate countries.

Manufacturing jobs are lost

The combination of fewer manufacturing jobs and lower wages is directly related to increased crime and the need for more police as we saw under item number (5) above in this chapter.

Industries lost to American workers

Many industries have been lost to American workers because of free trade and trade policies that do not protect American businesses and American workers. In the following list of industries mostly lost to American workers, either the American businesses have closed down or have moved their operations overseas due to the inability of making a reasonable profit with the high cost of American labor compared to the relative low cost of labor in Asia and countries south of the border such as Mexico.
Not only have these industries been lost to Americans forever but also the skills will be lost to new generations of Americans and opportunities for workers are lost forever.
The following list is only a partial list of all the industries that have been lost to America.

1. Textiles, blankets, rugs, and clothes manufacture.

2. Shoes.

3. Small tools.

4. Consumer electronics, television sets, sound equipment, cell phones, computers, printers, microwave ovens, etc.

5. General household items such as light bulbs, kitchen utensils, plastic containers, etc.

6. Furniture.

7. Appliances.

8. Ship building

In short, almost every industry that supplies easily transportable items has been virtually lost to American workers by imports from overseas factories. In many cases, the quality of products that was previously characteristic of most American made products is also now usually sub-standard and in many cases not even regulated by the government.

Some large industries are now threatened by foreign competition that has not been protected against by reasonable tariffs. These industries are heavy equipment, locomotives, and aircraft. A major example here is the commercial aircraft industry that has been severely penetrated by a massive foreign subsidized aircraft industry overseas.

The Automobile industry has safety issues due to sub-standard car and parts imports

The American auto industry has lost significant share of its market to cheaper foreign imports. Also, foreign automobile companies have established manufacturing plants in "right-to-work" states where American workers earn a lower wage than workers at the American car manufacturing plants. But at least, this situation still provides jobs for Americans.

Yes, the quality of American cars started to suffer in the early 1970's which opened the door to import cars which some people liked because they had better fuel economy and supposedly better quality.

Part of the quality problems with American cars in the 1970's was due to the imposition of government regulations requiring control of exhaust emissions.

As I am writing this book we have a case of massive automobile safety recalls because of deaths and injuries due to an allegedly faulty foreign piece of crash protection equipment. This recall has affected foreign and domestic automobiles on a gigantic scale. See link no. 38 for more information.

Link no. 38.

http://www.freep.com/story/money/cars/chrysler/2015/01/31/nhtsa-air-bag-recall/22648089/

Also certain foreign made automobiles were recently identified as cars that are most frequently involved in the cause of fatalities in accidents. See below.

The most unsafe automobiles

In a report by Chris Woodyard of USA Today, titled "New study reveals 10 cars most likely to kill you", dated January 30th, 2015, 10 cars have been found to have the highest death rates of vehicles on U.S. roads.
In the study, the top three vehicles were made by foreign companies and represented small, light-weight, inexpensive vehicles. Of the 10 cars reported, 6 of the 10 were foreign manufacture. For more information see link no. 39.

Link no. 39.
http://www.usatoday.com/story/money/cars/2015/01/29/iihs-driver-death-cars-top-10/22536459/

How can the safety problems with automobiles be solved?

Each vehicle and model that is certified for use on U.S. roads should be proven crash worthy and safe for occupants before it is allowed to be sold in the U.S. This should be true for American automobile manufacturers and for foreign manufacturers.

The quality of foreign made automobiles should also be verified as to durability and service life. Some foreign vehicles require high-dollar maintenance periodically to maintain the customer's warranty. This is a hidden cost of ownership and should be made illegal in the U.S.

Free trade has unintended consequences

The free trade with China has helped that nation tool its manufacturing base and build a military that is capable of manufacturing advanced fighter aircraft and military ships which now challenge the U.S. in international waters.

While China might not be considered our "enemy", we have shifted our military bases and positioning to counter the Chinese military threat. So this is an unintended consequence of the free trade with China. *We have helped the Chinese build up their military forces at the expense of loss of American jobs and whole industries!*

At the same time China often opposes the U.S. in the UN Security Council and is guilty of many human rights violations including the persecution of Christians. China is not a democratic country. China is a communist dictatorship. There is no reason that the U.S. should help China in any way, especially by free trade with them. The liberal-progressive politicians believe that free trade is supposed to make a country more democratic. There is no proof that this has ever worked. We have had free trade with China for many years, but they are still a communist dictatorship, and they will remain so unless the Chinese people rise up and throw out the communists.

The Trans-Pacific Partnership free trade agreement

A recent free trade agreement proposal is the "Trans-Pacific Partnership". This agreement will cover an area in the south pacific that encompasses approximately 40% of the world's economy! Supposedly the agreement will provide more markets for American manufacturers, but there is no way that manufacturing operations based in the U.S. will be able to compete with the low labor rates in Asian countries. It will simply mean that more U.S. companies will move operations into the newly opened low cost labor markets.
Of course all kinds of protections are promised for American business and labor, but is there really any way to trade with these low labor rate markets on a basis that is fair to American labor without the application of very high tariffs on foreign imports? See link 40 for more information on this agreement (The government's explanation.)

Link 40.

https://ustr.gov/tpp

Fair Trade

What is better than "free trade"? I propose "fair trade" programs. In fair trade, each country that is party to the agreement would be allowed to set tariffs that are fairly set so that the import competes fairly with the price and labor cost structure of the country when it is importing goods that compete with its own industries. The tariffs could be mutually agreed upon and subject to periodic review by a commission made up of representatives from each country that is a party to the trade agreement.
Whatever structure is decided upon, it should not be another do-good give away program dreamed up by far left liberals in the U.S. Congress.

Summary on the "Free Trade" problem

The multiple free trade programs the U.S. has engaged in has destroyed whole industries in the U.S., forced small businesses to close, caused the loss of many jobs, and caused high un-employment and high crime rates. Trillions of potential dollars of American wealth has been lost to foreign nations. Trillions of more dollars are held in foreign lands by large multi-national corporations that have been earned by the corporations but do not benefit Americans in any way.

Free trade is really an attempt by liberal far left politicians to give away American wealth on the premise that we are too rich and foreigners need our help. In fact, the only visible result of this naive liberal give-away program has been to build up the manufacturing base of our enemies to the detriment of our own military power.

Now we do not have enough commerce and business inside the U.S. to generate enough tax revenue to take care of U.S. needs such as repair of our infrastructure and taking care of the needs of the veterans, disabled, poor, and elderly people that are suffering without jobs and the barest of assistance.

We have had to cut back such vital programs as various kinds of weapons systems, aircraft, and ships. There is hardly any money for a manned space program, or funding for advanced scientific research.

America is in deep trouble because of the do-good free trade and foreign aid programs.

Chapter 6
Terrorism

Terror Attacks

According to *The Guardian* news in a blog article dated April 17, 2013, "Four decades of U.S. terror attacks listed and detailed", there have been about 2600 terror attacks of various types in the USA from 1970 to 2011. See link no. 3.

link no. 3
http://www.theguardian.com/news/datablog/2013/apr/17/four-decades-us-terror-attacks-listed-since-1970

Terrorism attacks are now a part of life in the USA, and the number and severity of attacks will probably increase over a period of time. Without any changes in the policies of the USA or changes in other countries of the world, terrorism attacks in the USA will continue for the foreseeable future and require more and more police to protect the public. This is another reason the American police state will come into existence.
Terrorists need to be dealt with at their origins along with their leaders before they invade the USA. This is a job for the military to do.
There is not only the possibility of violent physical attacks but also the real danger of the cyber attacks that the US is experiencing as I am writing this book. For example the attacks on Target, J.P. Morgan, Home Depot, Sony Pictures, and others.

The response to terrorism

What is the likely response to terrorism increasing in the USA? Of course it will be a continuing increase in the number of police, FBI agents, homeland security personnel, surveillance cameras, and electronic surveillance.

The NSA will no doubt continue to expand in its power to collect intelligence data on Americans and foreigners. In other words, a continuing expansion of the police state that is already in the process of forming in the USA.

In the case of terrorism, the main problem in apprehending and arresting terrorists before they commit their terrible acts is that under current laws they cannot be arrested unless a crime is committed or a plan or conspiracy is in evidence. Unfortunately, the only way that evidence is by way of surveillance, which means more police with more surveillance, thereby increasing the powers of the police and the NSA. Arrests can be made of the individuals who are instigating, or planning, or conspiring to commit terrorism.

But the price is the invasion of privacy of a lot of innocent individuals. The NSA must collect virtually all telephone conversations in order to find the few calls that are terrorist related!

So the question is this: Is catching a few terrorists worth the price of the loss of privacy of innocent law-abiding individuals? I believe that the answer is yes, if we are really concerned about terrorism. If you don't have anything to hide, then you have nothing to worry about, at least in the short term.

But the real problem is the expansion of police and NSA surveillance powers that can ultimately lead to police rule of the country. In other words, the creation of a police state dictatorship is a possible development in the U.S in the name of prevention of terrorist acts.

We must find and defeat terrorism as fast as possible with a minimum of resources and have very definite limits on police surveillance activities. At the same time, the NSA must have the ability to scan all communications for terrorist activity.

Teaching or advocating terrorism should be a crime

It seems like it should also be a crime to teach, preach or train people in a manner that incites, teaches, or advocates violence or terrorism against any group, religion, or peoples of the United States or its interests abroad, regardless of the location of the individuals. People are turned into terrorists by other people who advocate it, and by conditions that are creating a hatred for American society.

Of course the problem is that to find people who teach or preach terrorism requires heavy surveillance and even undercover agents or police to actually spy on teachers of religion. So this goes against the U.S. Constitution freedom of speech, and doing so would result in a large expansion of police powers.

The need for fast action

The longer terrorism is allowed to flourish and organize into larger and larger groups into tens of thousands of fighters and terrorists, the more the surveillance and police powers in America will grow along with it, as well as more and more American soldiers deployed overseas to fight the terrorists.
Therefore any large groups of terrorist fighters that form should be smashed as soon as possible by whatever military means necessary.
Otherwise, the terrorists will acquire more and more territory and more and more terrorists and fighters that will occupy new territory and also conduct terrorist acts around the world. To delay definitive action against such groups is to extend the war against them and also result in the expansion of surveillance and police powers.

Conditions that foster terrorism

The liberals will tell you that the conditions that foster terrorism are discrimination, poverty created by the lack of jobs for un-educated individuals, and racial and ethnic discrimination in the hiring process that is rampant in certain areas and within certain companies. These conditions certainly do not help, but in every major case of terrorism in the U.S., the terrorists were religious zealots of one kind or another

There is a vicious circle. Certain ethnic groups are discriminated against. They cannot get an education because they are poor and cannot afford the expensive college education. They cannot get jobs because they are not educated, and their children cannot get educated because the head of the family cannot get a job, mainly because they are discriminated against and they are uneducated. Then add in the preaching of extremist radical religion or association with radical peers and you have the basics to create terrorists.

It is well known for example, that certain "high technology" companies have a very low ratio of minorities relative to the majority of whites employed. Certainly the level of education is a factor here, and again we get back to the problem of poor education available to minorities in certain areas, especially those cities with poverty-stricken areas, with high crime and poor schools. But that is a problem that all minorities face, not just the religious zealots.

Young men become disaffected and dissatisfied with the economic problems and the discrimination that they face. In the case of a few, their disaffection will turn into hatred, making them fertile ground for recruiting into terrorist groups.

Defeating terrorism

Terrorism cannot be defeated by military or police force alone. Military and police forces can suppress, impede, or even prevent some terrorist actions. So military and police force against terrorism will continue and even increase with time. But there must also be an effort to correct the conditions that foster terrorism in the first place, especially discrimination, poor education, a lack of job opportunities, the resulting poverty, and most of all the radicalization of young men by preachers or religious leaders who spout radical religious extremism.

The people who advocate and teach terrorism must be rooted out of society. Yes, the U.S. allows free speech, but when it is really a conspiracy to promote terrorism by teaching or advocating such actions, that should be a severe criminal offense punishable by death or life imprisonment.

How do we root out the teaching of terrorism? Unfortunately there is no complete and sure way. We can only apply the methods of undercover surveillance and the monitoring of suspicious groups and individuals. At the same time we must be careful to respect free speech as guaranteed under the constitution.

The "acid test" is whether or not the radical teachings of religious zealots advocate the overthrow of the U.S. government and are therefore guilty of conspiracy. Here again we see one of the forces that will tend to move the U.S. further in the direction of the police state. So we must be very careful in the use of such powers. There should always be a warrant approved by a federal judge for any surveillance activities carried out inside the United States.

We must also get at the root causes of terrorism, arresting the conspirators that advocate terrorism against the U.S.

The other things we can do is in the area of better education, stimulating business to create more jobs, and making an effective effort to raise the standard of living for all Americans.

Terrorism is now a fact of life

But terrorism will probably be a part of this world's foreseeable future for a long time to come as long as people are recruited by extremist religious zealots and have the will to resist the terrorist's desire to kill and take over territory. However there are other things that can be done to try to reduce terrorism. We should fight the ideological battle-- in other words, we should attack the extremist ideology regardless of what religion it stems from or who supports it.

Fighting the ideological battle

America must make it clear that we do not battle any religion, but only the radical extremist ideology that advocates attacks against the U.S, and the resulting terrorism, regardless of the religion or source of the problem. But we should always say who is responsible and what the source of the terrorism is. At the same time we must clean our sheets of wrong doings such as mistreatment of prisoners and torture, with a clear restatement of our democratic ideals. We should pass strong laws against prisoner mistreatment and torture. We must show by example that we are changing our ways, and that we practice our beliefs in accordance with the U.S. Constitution.

The terrorists fight us with terrorist acts, weapons and propaganda. Our response should be better weapons, better strategic planning, punishing strikes, and yes, better propaganda, but the propaganda of truth, not lies.

Show our new policies by way of example

One way to show our new policies are going to be followed is to close the "gitmo" prison and move the detainees into our regular military prison system after due process of military court martial. One such prison is Fort Leavenworth. There they can treated like any other military prisoner, and the most dangerous individuals can be placed in the maximum security prison located there.

Terrorists should be either executed or imprisoned for life. They have demonstrated their violence and they cannot be trusted to have freedom at any time.

Using the power of propaganda against terrorists

Lately the terror groups have been using social media to spread their message and post propaganda messages. They are also producing slick paper publications to spread far and wide. We must counter this with our own propaganda-- showing people that there is a better way of life and opportunity based on the freedom and ideals of democracy without discrimination against race or religion.
We can use television, radio, the social media, and the printed word to get out our message.

The hazards of surveillance and additional police required to control terrorism

The downside is that the increased surveillance and police required to find and arrest terrorists also increases the power of the police and moves the country further towards the police state condition. So, there has to be tight civilian control over the operations in terms of limiting the police powers in accordance with the Constitution.

Judges can improve the handling of search warrants

Judges will still be needed to approve and issue warrants, but this process should be handled quickly and efficiently with the oversight of the state legislature to make sure judges do not exceed their authority or demand excessive constraints on the police, delaying operations. Each state should have a law which governs the issue of warrants, with clear and simple criteria to make a decision whether or not to issue a warrant, a quick and simple process. For example, the police can fill out a standard form with a check-list of criteria, submit it to the judge, and all the judge has to do is sign it to make it official.

Terrorism could force the creation of the police state

If authorities are unable to apprehend and incarcerate terrorists, under existing constitutional law, before they commit their acts of terrorism, then the far right could take power and create a police state where anyone can be incarcerated or even executed just on someone's say so or even trumped up evidence, that they are a terrorist or an "enemy of the state".
We must guard closely against this possibility and be vigilant in protecting our rights under the U.S. Constitution.

An example of the increase of police and surveillance because of terrorist acts

The terror attacks on the office of Charlie Hebdo and the attack on the Jewish market in Paris on January 7, the policewoman killing on January 8, and the supermarket attack on January 9, 2015 (see link no. 41), has sparked a massive police and surveillance program in France (see link no. 42.)

Link no. 41. "Charlie Hebdo attack: Three days of terror", *BBC News Europe*.

http://www.bbc.com/news/world-europe-30708237

Link no. 42. "France anti-terror plan calls for hiring more intel agents"-- *Associated Press* via *cnsnews.com*

Link 42.

http://cnsnews.com/news/article/france-anti-terror-plan-calls-hiring-more-intel-agents

France's response to the Paris terrorist attack shows how police and surveillance powers will expand as a result of terror.

Illegal immigration and its relation to terrorism

Illegal immigration solutions

The immigration problem can be fixed mainly by reducing requirements for entry, speeding up processing of applications, and tightening border security. There is plenty of room for legal immigrants in the United States (if they are tax payers) and there is no good reason at this time to hold back good people who want to come here and work, who do not have criminal backgrounds, and are healthy.

But we do have to be concerned about terrorist elements sneaking across our borders with Mexico and Canada. This is one of the reasons that we need good protection of our borders against illegal border crossings by persons unknown as to their criminal records and their possible terrorist activities inside the U.S.

Our internet infrastructure needs work to make it more secure against cyber attacks

Recently we have seen our enemies launch cyber attacks against us. These attacks will only get more frequent and deadly as time progresses. A heavy cyber attack that affects infrastructure, such as our power grids, will be almost as devastating as a nuclear attack. If our country suffers a devastating cyber attack, there may be chaos and a sharp increase in criminal activity. The result will no doubt be the application of more police power, and possibly even martial law (See Link A for the number of police by country including the USA.) Our freedoms will be seriously reduced and the military or police could take over the government producing the new American police state!

Will our low spending on education and science really be sufficient to prepare our military to protect us against cyber warfare?

Summary

In summary, terrorism is now a major problem for the U.S. and the world and is a very large threat to freedom of speech and other freedoms. The major problem for the free world will be to combat terrorism without massive growth in police and government surveillance powers that will threaten to engulf the free countries of the world turning them into nations controlled by all-powerful police organizations, especially in the U.S. where police power has been growing steadily and where the NSA and other government agencies are already conducting massive world-wide surveillance. The reach of the FBI has expanded in recent years even to the point of being a potent force overseas.

Police agencies of various European countries are now talking about better coordination between their police and intelligence services, recent examples being the cooperation between U.S. and French police authorities, and now between the Scandinavian countries and the rest of Europe.

Terrorism will only add pressure to the increase of the police powers of the U.S. and the free world to even more massive and potent forces with great influence over civilian authorities, and maybe someday the absolute power of a police dictatorship in the U.S. and elsewhere.

Chapter 7
Government anti-business policies and problems related to government laws and practices

In recent years U.S. government policies have been largely anti-business. Examples are the heavy corporate taxes, the Dodd-Frank law, the "net neutrality" ruling, insider trading prosecutions, and government lawsuits against legitimate business based on questionable complaints. See link 43.

Link 43.
http://en.wikipedia.org/wiki/Dodd%E2%80%93Frank_Wall_Street_Reform_and_Consumer_Protection_Act

Net neutrality

A good example is the so-called "net neutrality" plan fostered by the FCC. In the guise of more freedom of the internet, the government is actually applying the old rules of the old telephone industry regulations. For example, an internet service provider could not charge more for high speed service than for the ordinary speed service. Such rules remove the business incentive to build new and faster networks for business and commerce. So the so-called "net neutrality" plan would better be called "net stagnation"!

The war on the rich

There is also the "war on the rich" going on without being named as such but being applied on the theory of "spreading the wealth", or "leveling the playing field", or "leveling the masses", an old far left socialist dream.
There is the thought in the far left liberal ranks that no one should be as rich as some of the richest Americans such as Bill Gates or Warren Buffet, even though these men have contributed greatly to the wealth and power of America.

What do the rich contribute to society?

It has been said that every time a man becomes a millionaire, at least 10 new jobs are created. But now the Federal Reserve Board has diluted the value of the dollar so much that being a millionaire is almost nothing and you really have to be a billionaire to a rich person. In any case the very rich do create a lot of jobs and purchase a lot of goods and services which helps to increase the GDP, the Gross Domestic Product.

Why does the government want to tax the rich at a heavier rate?

So why is the government set on bring the rich down by taxing them at even higher rates and working against big business? It is because the typical far left liberal politician in Congress and the White House believes they are helping the "common man" by fighting business and the rich. *In fact the reverse is true. Making it harder for businesses to grow and flourish hurts the "common man" because fewer jobs are created and the pay will be low because of the regulations and tax burdens placed on small and large businesses by the far left politicians!*

What happens if fewer people are rich due to government taxes and regulations?

Fewer rich people in the country will translate into lower retail sales and commerce, and thus fewer new jobs will be available. Economic recession will be the rule instead of economic prosperity.
Increased taxes on rich citizens will motivate them to leave the U.S. to live in foreign countries where taxes on the rich are lower.

Rich men are often innovators and creators of business and wealth

Where would the U.S. be today if it were not for the wealthy industrialists like Andrew Carnegie, John D. Rockefeller, J. P. Morgan, Cornelius Vanderbilt, Henry Ford, and others of the past? Yes some of these men became rich by hard work and being innovators, but some were rich by inheritance, notably J. P. Morgan.

The rich innovators of today

Today we have the rich drivers of innovation and technology like Elon Musk (Tesla Motors and Space X), Larry Ellison (Oracle Corp.), Bill Gates (Microsoft, retired), Mark Zuckerberg (Facebook), Richard Branson (Virgin Galactic Corp.), and others.
These rich people in the U.S. are the drivers of innovation and new businesses, or they have become rich by being innovators and creators of new businesses. Should these people now be punished by higher taxes when they have added to the wealth and power of America?

We should not drive our rich away with high taxes

To lose people like these major rich industrialists to other countries would mean a great loss of jobs in the U.S.

We already know that fewer jobs and lower wages are the precursor to a higher crime rate and the resulting expansion of police forces and powers.

Should higher wages be forced on business?

Lately there has been pressure by liberals to increase the minimum wage.
Wages should be set by market forces-- that is, the supply and demand for labor. If the environment for business is good (relatively unfettered by government regulations) and the economy is doing well with intelligent and reasonable government policies, then there should be a good market for workers, and workers with good qualifications will find good paying jobs.

Most companies already pay more than minimum wage

In many cases businesses pay higher wages than the minimum wage to their lowest paid workers. The latest example is the giant store chain Wal-Mart which is scheduled to set their lowest wages above the minimum wage. Why is Wal-Mart doing this? Because Wal-Mart, like so many other businesses, knows that they must pay a competitive wage to attract the best workers.

A flourishing economy will create a competitive job market

A company that wants competent workers will pay higher wages in a competitive job market, but of course that company will also expect the workers to have a minimum degree of education and perhaps experience and special skills for some jobs.
Flourishing business that is not over-taxed and over-regulated will support a competitive job market and foster higher wages for people.

Education is the key to employment

But people who have not completed their minimum education requirements, have not learnt any skills, or have not had any job training, or did not learn anything in school due to a poor education, will find the job market is hard to break into. Again we get back to the importance of education and job training!

High government taxes and regulations can be a cause of crime

In a vicious cycle, liberal government politicians force high taxes and regulations on business, bringing on business recessions and high unemployment rates. An increase in crime is the result. More police and prison cells are required, and therefore taxes and regulations must be increased even further. More and more people are pushed into poverty by the liberal do-gooders who unfortunately do not realize what they are doing is making a bad situation even worse. The possibility of the development of the police state becomes more and more likely.

Government Spending

The US government spends money in ways that are almost exactly backward to what the spending priorities should be. Below is a simplified list of the president's proposed budget for 2015, according to a report by the *National Priorities Project* titled "Federal Spending: Where Does the Money Go, Federal Budget 101". You can read the full report at link no. 44.

link no. 44.
https://www.nationalpriorities.org/budget-basics/federal-budget-101/spending/

Here are a few items from the discretionary portion of the proposed budget I mention here:

Military spending 55%
Education 6%

Welfare items, housing, community, medicine, Social Security, Unemployment, Labor 15% (items lumped together from the above referenced report.)
Science 3%
Transportation 2%

Now let's consider the above data to see what the implications are. First of all military spending is almost 10 times the spending on education. Welfare spending is 3 times as much as education. Spending on science is less than one-tenth of military spending.
A little thought should tell you that there is something wrong with the priorities here.

The effect of military spending

Dwight D. Eisenhower (a republican) could not have said it better when he said,

"Every gun that is made, every warship launched, every rocket fired, signifies in the final sense a theft from those who hunger and are not fed, those who are cold and are not clothed."

There is no doubt that wars drain the country of resources and wealth. Domestic spending on infrastructure and essential social programs such as education suffer as a result.

What should be the real priority in government spending?

Education should be the number one priority in this country because we can do nothing well without a good education for our people. Here there will be disagreement from the right side of the political spectrum.
You will hear objections like "The kids don't want to learn. They just want to sit home and watch video games!" (Someone actually said that to me!) Or they will say something like "It's the parents fault that the kids don't study and learn!" Of course there are always children that will not do well in school no matter what you do. It is not always the parent's fault. As a father who has raised two children I can testify to that!

Free tuition for all Americans for two years of community college?

A recent proposal of President Obama is to have a system of free tuition for two years for all American students. Although this program will be expensive, I believe that this program is very much needed and pay huge dividends in terms of the productivity, lowering of crime, and improving the wealth and economic power of the United States. But as usual, with most government programs, the program is poorly conceived and lacks basic needs of the people.

A real educational program for the people beyond high school should include vocational training as well as academic training. Some people do not want or need academic training but they do want vocational training that is of immediate practical use in terms of finding a job. Vocational training should include many skills that are sorely needed today. Here is a partial list of training that could be included and would provide high paying jobs to Americans:

1. Aircraft maintenance.

2. Automotive mechanics.

3. Computer aided manufacturing.

4. Computer operators and programming.

5. Construction trades, such as carpenter, plumber, HVAC, electrician, brick-layer, etc.

6. Machining and welding.

7. Robotics technician.

Public Education

Are teachers really qualified?

But if the teachers are not really qualified due to lack of proper training, or if they are not properly helping students and motivating them to learn, or if the school facility is so old fashioned and run down it looks something like Alcatraz, how can we expect kids to come out of the public school system motivated and with a good education?

Who should be responsible for educating children?

Others will say "It should be up to the state where the schools are located to educate kids, not the Federal government!" Yes each individual state bears responsibility for education of its population. And that should not be a problem if the state is rich enough and has the expertise for the task. But there are a lot of poor states that need help, not only with money, but also with expert help which could be provided by the Federal government. But I am not letting states off the hook for the responsibility of educating their people! They certainly are primarily responsible! Of course it is also true that the states or the federal government cannot solve every problem.

One thing is clear, and that is that the federal government should not dictate any rules, tests, or achievement levels to the states. Each state should set their own standards.

What do teachers need to do to get American children educated?

The most important thing for teachers to do to get children educated is to first get them motivated to learn! This means that classroom teaching should be interesting, stimulating and exciting for children.
If children can get interested in something, this is the way to open the door to their minds. The second thing to do is to try to get students to understand that if they want to have a career, or a good job, they must be persistent in reaching their goal. This means not giving up, not dropping out of school without a diploma, overcoming obstacles, and pursuing their goal with grit and gusto!

What is missing in education of American children in the higher grades?

There are a lot of big gaping holes in American public education through the high school level, especially in the area of mathematics and science. One course that is really needed is the teaching of information technology skills, including hardware and software. We are living in an age where anyone who is not computer literate will not be in a position to get higher paying jobs.

Also very important are the non-academic skills such as construction, plumbing, electrician work, automotive mechanics, machining, heating, ventilation, and air conditioning (HVAC.) This kind of teaching is best done by trade schools that are available to students as an alternative to academic training. All high schools should have a local trade school facility for this training.

If America is to grow, prosper, and have plenty of good paying jobs for workers, students must be properly trained in the kind of work they want to do!

Another problem with high school education today is that students do learn anything about financial matters.

For example, why should a worker save for retirement? What should be a good savings rate? Ten per cent of salary? Fifteen per cent? Twenty per cent?

How should a worker save money for retirement? A savings account? An investment program? Stocks and bonds? Real estate?

Students need financial education so that at retirement they do not need so much government assistance or welfare. Also if a family has been saving money it is more likely that their children will be able to attend college. People need education to be successful and be able to send their children to college.

A smarter and better educated America is a stronger and more competitive America!

But most important of all is that educated Americans are more likely to have good jobs with good pay and therefore less likely to become criminals!

What effect does education have on the American military?

Now what is the quality of our military troops and our weapons going to be if we don't have people that are well educated?
Where are we going to get the engineers and scientists to do military design and development work if we don't have an educated public? We certainly cannot get military workers from any foreign countries that are potential enemies or security risks!

How does education affect employment and the crime problem?

Now if people are better educated there will be more jobs with higher pay available to them, so the conclusion is that education is one of the major keys to solving the crime problem. Quoting from the report above again:

"From 1979 to 1997, federal statistics show the inflation-adjusted wages of men without a college education fell by 20 percent.

Despite declines after 1993, the property and violent crime rates (adjusted for changes in the country's demographics) increased by 21 percent and 35 percent respectively during that period."

A strong relationship between jobs, wages, and crime

So the study shows that there is a strong relationship between jobs, wages, and the crime rate. But should we then raise the minimum wage? See the next section for a discussion of the minimum wage.

Job Availability and its Relation to Crime

More jobs available for people means less crime! A lack of jobs results in an abundance of crime! A lack of jobs means that there is an excess of applicants for any given job. This means that the wages paid on fewer jobs will be lower because of the law of supply and demand-- that is economics 101 (unless a strong union is protecting wages, but then such plants controlled by unions will force management to hire as few workers as possible.)

Unemployment and low wages are related to crime

A study was done at Ohio State University that showed that unemployment and low wages especially are related to the crime rate. Bruce Weinberg, co-author of the study and associate professor of economics at Ohio State University said:

"Public officials can put more cops on the beat, pass tougher sentencing laws, and take other steps to reduce crime, but there are limits to how much these [steps] can do," he said. "We found that a bad labor market has a profound impact on the crime rates."

A report from *Research News* on the study can be found at link no. 45.

link no. 45.
http://researchnews.osu.edu/archive/crimwage.htm

Welfare

Why are welfare expenses so high?

Welfare expenses are high because so many people have not had a good enough education to earn enough money to provide for themselves and their families. The do not qualify for good jobs so they can support themselves, or in some cases people cannot work because of physical or mental disabilities. Also employers are very unlikely to hire people who have physical or mental disabilities, and of course this is another form of discrimination in the US. But the US lawmakers, particularly liberal US lawmakers, insist on spending more money on welfare than education to reduce the need for welfare! Entitlements are getting close to eating up the entire budget!

Is the discretionary proposed budget really what America needs?

In any case it is fairly obvious with a little thought that the proposed discretionary budget is not really what this country needs to solve the joblessness, poverty, and crime problems that is turning this country into a police state.

Will American technology be affected by science spending?

And how good is our technology going to be, and what knowledge will we be missing that we need in the future, if we only spend 3% of the budget on science? In the final overall budget plan the money for science drops to 1%. This is really totally short-sighted planning!
Important innovations come from scientific research and many times these innovations create

new jobs and help reduce un-employment, thus reducing the crime problem.

Also some of the military's best weapons are based on scientific research. Examples are night vision, laser guided weapons, radar, nuclear powered ships and submarines, not to mention nuclear weapons, and a host of other military devices and hardware that are based on the results of scientific research.

No I don't advocate the use of nuclear weapons, but the genie has been let out of the bottle. Now our enemies have them and maintain them, and so we must maintain them also.

Should America spend money on military weapons?

Yes, spend enough money on improved weapons, missiles and aircraft. We need the high technology weapons, and military work does create jobs. But do we need to spend 55% on the military, or can the military budget be reduced, and the savings applied to higher priority things such as improving our educational system, job training, and making infrastructure improvements? Let's build a smarter more efficient military with reduced manpower needs and better capability *to respond quickly* wherever American military force is needed! *We also need to increase the science research budget so that the results of more scientific research can be applied towards better and smarter military weapons!*

What about our infrastructure?

Where is the money for our decaying infrastructure? Yes there is 2% for "transportation", but we need a lot more money for infrastructure to keep our nation from total decay and ultimate weakness like "third world" countries.

A decaying infrastructure is related to increased crime because of its deleterious effect on business and the discouraging effects on people's perceptions of the quality of their lives in urban environments. If you don't believe this assertion, ask yourself if you would want to live in a city that has decaying roads and bridges? Would you buy a house there? Would you start a business there that would create jobs for people? Would you be happy if your children went to schools with decaying buildings and inadequate facilities?

Should the federal government pay for all infrastructure improvements? No, but some help for the poorer states and communities is in order.

The effect of poor infrastructure on defense of the homeland

Another problem is related to military defense of our country in the event of invasion by a foreign power (yes it is becoming possible with advancing technology and the military build-ups in the countries of our enemies.) Our military needs good roads and rail transportation to quickly move troops and equipment across the country to wherever the weapons and troops may be needed for defense. Dwight D. Eisenhower realized this was a problem and he started the Interstate Highway program which has been a big boost to our infrastructure and military transportation needs. But more work is needed for new interstate highways and better roads and rail lines. High speed rail is definitely needed in USA. Other countries already have it. Why don't we have it?

What does infrastructure spending have to do with the crime problem?

Properly maintaining our infrastructure improves our quality of life and creates jobs for workers, helping to reduce the number of people who will turn to crime due to a lack of jobs for them.

So poor infrastructure is related to a poor job market and people who live in such cities will find it hard to find a decent job! Infrastructure work provides good jobs for people, improves the quality of life in the community, increases the number of businesses that employ people, and helps to reduce the crime problem as a benefit.

Infrastructure work should be a continuous job in USA, not the sporadic and temporary efforts we have seen so far in our history.

America needs a jobs program

In any American city of large size that you look at there are large areas of the city that are essentially low-income slums. People who live there are trapped in poverty. The schools are poor and the education is poor. There are no jobs available for these people. America needs an emergency solution to this problem.

I know that conservative politicians will not like this idea, but the government needs to do whatever is necessary to find or create jobs and job skills training for these people, even if it is "make-work" projects. Yes that is a "liberal" idea straight from the era of Franklin Delano Roosevelt! But we have an emergency right now. But there are plenty of needed projects to repair and improve our infrastructure, such as repair and up-dating our roads and bridges.

We need high speed rail as an alternative to the crowded air space travel and the out-dated interstate system of roads. We need the construction of nuclear power plants so that we do not have to burn carbon dioxide producing fossil fuels just to generate power. Also the government can support the construction of renewable energy projects such as wind farms and solar energy farms to eventually replace nuclear fission plants and coal burning facilities. In addition to the up-dating of our infrastructure, we need to put more emphasis on the development of fusion power as the ultimate way to generate clean power with the minimum usage of land that may be needed for agricultural purposes some day.

So as we can see there are plenty of worthwhile projects that can be tackled with government help or subsidies to create jobs and work for people at all levels of education.

Crime and the police are almost out of control. Something drastic needs to be done.

Putting a man to work is a lot better than paying him welfare!

Granted, a better way is to stimulate business to create meaningful jobs. But can we wait for the anti-business liberals to help conservatives create a pro-business government? Will that ever happen in our extremely partisan government?

The Minimum Wage laws

Wages should be set by market forces-- that is, the supply and demand for labor. If the environment for business is good (relatively unfettered by government regulations) and the economy is doing well with intelligent and reasonable government policies, then there should be a good market for workers, and workers with good qualifications will find good paying jobs.

But people who have not completed their education requirements, have not learned any skills, or have not had any job training, or did not learn anything in school due to a poor education, will find the job market is hard to break into. Again we get back to the importance of education and job training!

The minimum wage can slow job creation

The minimum wage is a disaster for jobs creation. Why? The reason is that every time the minimum wage is raised, businesses that hire people will do one or more of several things:

Businesses will raise qualifications

a) Businesses will raise the qualifications for jobs regardless of the type of work that is required. So a lot of people will not be able to get a job because even the lowest level jobs will require a high school diploma or higher education, as well as experience. Existing employees will find it harder to get raises because they have already been raised to the new minimum wage, and their qualifications will now likely be less than that of new employees coming in with the newly required higher qualifications.

Employers will load jobs with more required work

b) Employers will make sure that the higher paid workers will have more extensive job descriptions, and will be required to work even harder to get their jobs done each day. The employer will want to "get his monies worth" out of each and every hourly worker that is employed at the new minimum wage!

Hiring will slow down and some businesses will reduce employment

c) A lot of employers will stop hiring new workers and some will actually reduce their employment levels with "cutbacks" or sometimes referred to as "rifs" (reduction in force.) Or management will simply eliminate certain jobs, and load other employees with any extra work that results. So this is a very direct way that increasing the minimum wage will produce increases in unemployment.

Employers will take steps to cut labor costs

d) If an employer must pay a higher wage, then he will look for other ways to save on the labor costs. For example, some benefits such as health insurance, vacation time, and any other benefits that involve cost to the employer may be cut back or even eliminated. So the employee may not really experience any gain from the increased minimum wage, and even maybe lose more than what was gained!

Businesses will raise prices

e) Employers will raise the price of their products or services to their customers wherever possible. So the minimum wage can be a driver for inflation, and workers do not really gain much from the wage increases because their expenses for food and other necessities will increase also.

The minimum wage hurts small businesses the most

Large businesses will find ways to cut costs or reduce the number of people they employ, but small businesses that are already struggling every day to stay in business, will simply go out of business and lay off all employees.
Small business suffers the most from the minimum wage law. Some people who would like to go into business for themselves will decide not to, because the high cost of labor will not allow them to run a profitable business, unless they can do all of the work themselves.

American goods become more expensive than foreign goods

The minimum wage is also a disaster because it makes American products more expensive than foreign goods, so American exports fall and jobs related to foreign trade will disappear. Examples of industries that have been lost or decimated to American workers because of lower labor rates in other countries: textiles, consumer electronics, electronic parts, assembly operations, tools, small appliances, and a lot of other items and services.

Older people will find it harder to find work

Finally, a lot of jobs traditionally filled by older people such as janitorial work, housemaids, gardeners, and other simple low level jobs will be taken by desperate younger people. It will be very hard on older American citizens who still need jobs to survive.

The Federal Reserve Board causes economic problems which increases crime

Does the Federal Reserve really protect our money supply?

The Federal Reserve Board has not been a good steward of the U.S. dollar. At one time, a 1 troy ounce gold coin with a $20 face value was actually worth $20. Another way to think about it is to say that a $1 cash bill was worth 0.05 ounces of gold (1/20 of a troy ounce.) Now $1 is only worth about 0.000843 troy ounces of gold!

So what does this mean? Has gold really increased in value so much?

Has the value of gold increased?

No the value of gold has not increased-- the value of the U.S. dollar has been allowed to drop to almost nothing!
If you doubt this, some older people can tell you when they could buy a gallon of gasoline for 30 cents instead of $3, and a loaf of bread for 15 cents instead of $1.50 or more.

The value of the US dollar has been allowed to drop to almost a worthless amount

In other words the value of the U.S. dollar has been allowed to fall, and fall some more in almost every recent U.S. government administration. The Federal Reserve itself blatantly approves of an inflation rate of 2% per year. If you have had a bank savings account lately, you know that it is hard to get a savings rate above 2% so your savings account paying say 1.5% interest is actually losing your money!

Losing money in a savings account

So if you have a savings account, you are actually losing money as the value of the U.S. dollar continues to fall. Why does the dollar continue to fall? The primary reason is that the government prints money in excess of what the growth of the economy warrants.

In other words, if the Gross National Product grows by only 2%, the government should not be expanding the money supply in excess of 2%. But politicians cry for "financial stimulus" on every little recession that comes along, and the Federal Reserve bows easily to the pressure.

The Fed prints too much money

In an article by Dave Schwartz of the Washington Times, titled "The Feds Keep on Printing money", we read that in 2012 the government was printing 40 billion dollars a month to buy mortgage bonds of questionable if not worthless value. The full article can be read at link no. 46.

Link no. 46.
http://www.washingtontimes.com/news/2012/sep/26/the-fed-keeps-on-printing-money/

What effect has this had on America over the years?

People who thought they were saving enough money for retirement found out that there savings were not enough, and although they worked hard all of their lives, they were still poor at retirement age and their families remained poor. So why is this important to this book? It is important because the dropping of the value of savings and the inflation of prices has been a factor in perpetuating poverty in America and therefore is one of the factors that are at the basis of crime.

Why is inflation dangerous and how can it affect crime?

If the value of U.S. currency continues to fall, there could be a point where inflation becomes un-controllable, and chaos reins as people lose faith in U.S. currency. If chaos does occur, of course there will be a need for a great expansion of the police force and this could be the next step to creating the American police state.

Illegal Immigration

The liberals and the liberal press do not like the term "illegal immigrants."
They prefer the politically correct term "undocumented immigrants." Whatever you call them, they got here by illegal means unless they were born in the United States!

The Obama executive order on illegal immigrants

As of the 21st of November 2014, President Obama issued an executive order which stops the deportation of "undocumented immigrants" who

have been in the country more than 5 years, and allows a temporary work visa for up to 3 years, if people come forward and apply.
However the program has been held up in Federal Court as I am writing this book.

How does illegal immigration contribute to the crime problem?

How does illegal immigration contribute to the crime problem and to expansion of the police state? Many illegal immigrants are hard working and law abiding members of American society. Unfortunately there are also many illegal immigrants who are also criminals guilty of violent crimes, and they will most likely continue their criminal careers in USA!

How many illegal immigrants are criminals?

According to the *Center for Immigration Studies*, in a report titled "ICE Document Details 36,000 Criminal Alien Releases in 2013", by Jessica Vaughan, May 2014, there were over 36,000 criminals that were released from custody by the ICE in 2013. Quoting from the report: "This group included aliens convicted of hundreds of violent and serious crimes, including homicide, sexual assault, kidnapping, and aggravated assault."
Included in the crimes that these criminals were guilty of, were more than 16,000 convictions for

drunk or drugged driving. See link no. 47 for the full report.

Link no. 47.
http://cis.org/ICE-Document-Details-36000-Criminal-Aliens-Release-in-2013

Horrible crimes have been committed by illegal immigrants

A report by Townhall.com details 7 "horrible" crimes committed by illegal aliens. The list and description (which I do not want to repeat here) can be found at link no. 48.

Link no. 48.
http://townhall.com/columnists/johnhawkins/2014/05/20/7-horrible-crimes-committed-in-america-by-illegal-aliens-n1840468/page/full

America needs to control illegal immigration

Yes, it is true that legal citizens commit "horrible crimes" also. It is also true that most illegal aliens are not criminals (except that they may drive without a driver's license), so what is the point? The point is that that the illegal alien criminals would not have gotten into the country to commit their crimes if we had control over immigration in America.

What kind of legal immigration policy should the government put into effect?

America needs to grow its economy and will need more people to operate businesses and factories. Our birth rate is not high enough and our population is aging. We need fresh young people to boost out economy. At the same time the government has to reduce taxes and regulations on business so that an environment friendly to new business and innovation is created. Then America will grow and there will be good high paying jobs available. But we will need immigrants to work and fill the job positions.

A policy on immigration should be simplified so that any healthy individual that has a basic high school education is eligible to be an immigrant with only a few restrictions.

Immigrants should be non-aligned with known political or terrorist organizations that are against the United States, and immigrants should swear allegiance to the United States upon entry.

An immigrant who serves in the U.S. armed forces for at least one tour of duty should be eligible to become a citizen upon discharge without the usual test requirements.

America became a major industrial power in the early 1900's because of a liberal immigration policy at the time.

Why should we do this? The main reason is that we need to grow our economy and population to be competitive in the world market place and be able to export goods and services that can compete with any country. A bigger, stronger American economy will create more job availability and higher paying jobs that will reduce crime and reduce the number of police required per capita.

Over Regulation and Taxation of Business

When a country needs more jobs for its available work eligible population, it does not make sense for that government to add more regulations and taxes on businesses. The more expenses a business has, and the more restrictions it has on doing business, the slower its growth will be, and it will tend to hire fewer people to compensate for its extra costs of doing business because of government regulations and taxation.
The federal and state governments need to reduce taxes and regulations of business to the minimum so that business can flourish and many new jobs can be created!

The country with the highest tax rate on corporations

America presently has the highest tax on corporations of any major country in the world. Fig. 2, shows the U.S. Federal Income Tax Rate Schedule for U.S. corporations. It does not include state income taxes that also apply in some states.

Tax Rate Schedule

If taxable income (line 30, Form 1120) on page 1 is:

Over—	But not over—	Tax is:	Of the amount over—
$0	$50,000	15%	$0
50,000	75,000	$7,500 + 25%	50,000
75,000	100,000	13,750 + 34%	75,000
100,000	335,000	22,250 + 39%	100,000
335,000	10,000,000	113,900 + 34%	335,000
10,000,000	15,000,000	3,400,000 + 35%	10,000,000
15,000,000	18,333,333	5,150,000 + 38%	15,000,000
18,333,333	-----	35%	0

Fig. 2, U.S. Corporate Income Tax Rate Schedule Form 1120, for 2013

Example of how federal income taxes affect a small business

Suppose you own your own business and it earned a profit of $100,000 in 2013. You would have to pay a federal tax of $22,250 which reduces your net after taxes to $77,750. Now are you going to hire a new worker at a minimum wage of $7.25 an hour?

If you hired a new employee for full time 40 hours per week for one year (52 weeks), it would cost you at least $15,080 just in wages, not counting any benefits such as health insurance. If you did hire an employee, and assuming your business does not increase, then your income before taxes drops to $84,920 and you still have to pay a federal income tax of approximately $17,123, so your net after taxes is now $67,797 and your income is approaching lower middle class earnings.

You might decide to go out of business, laying off your employees and finding a job that pays you more money because taxes on businesses are so high!

Federal income tax is tough on small business

The conclusion is that the U.S. Federal Income tax rate is very tough on small business. Only if you own a very large business and your business generates more than $18,333,333 does your income tax rate flatten to 35%. But the 35% rate is still very onerous and you will have to keep the number of employees as low as possible to reduce your expenses.

Taxes and regulations reduce employment opportunities

The American corporations that do multi-national business are storing earnings made overseas in foreign countries instead of bringing the money home where they could use the money to create new products, do research, build new office buildings, or manufacturing plants, thereby providing more jobs for Americans.
The amount of money kept overseas to avoid U.S. corporate taxes is estimated to be $2.1 *trillion* dollars, according to an article by Adam Shell in *USA Today* titled "Tax proposal could cost Apple $10", February 3rd, 2015.
So, taxes and excessive regulations on businesses actually reduce employment opportunities, contribute to joblessness, and therefore lead to more criminal activity.

High taxes increase the power and scale of the police state

More criminal activity requires more police and a larger judicial to fight crime. The police state grows and becomes stronger with more and more political influence! The extra taxes the government collects on corporations is eaten away at by the necessity to increase the size of the FBI and local police forces. *So taxes are increased further to fight crime in a vicious cycle pushing the state towards a totalitarian regime controlled by the police and judicial system.*

The "Fair Tax" proposal

The so-called "fair tax" system that has been proposed, would replace all income taxes with a "consumption tax", or in other words a tax on all retail sales. But this is even worse than the present income tax system, because it unfairly penalizes the poor with small incomes that will pay a high percentage of their income on necessities such as food, clothes and other consumables.
A person with high income, or a rich person, on the other hand spends a low proportion of his income on necessities such as food and clothes. So the so-called "fair tax" would only increase the burdens on the poor and probably add to the crime problem by increasing poverty in the USA.

The anti-fossil fuel policy of the federal government

America has tremendous resources in coal, natural gas, and shale oil. At the present time, the renewable energy infrastructure is in its infancy and cannot yet support the energy needs of the country. For a long time we could not produce enough oil to fuel our transportation needs, and we were dependent on OPEC for a large part of our oil needs. Now, however we have a chance to become oil independent if we can bring in enough shale oil production.

But the government and the environmentalist lobby have done everything in their power to impede the progress of our domestic oil drilling companies. It is as if the government and the environmentalists do not care if we are held hostage to the OPEC criminal oligarchy or not! Now we also can get more oil from Canada if the Keystone Xl pipeline is built. As of this writing, Congress passed a law authorizing the pipeline but the President vetoed the bill.

If the government would drop its opposition to our oil drilling industry and to the extra oil from the Keystone XL pipeline, we can become oil independent!

Our domestic oil drilling industry needs government support by means of reduced taxes, and policies that reward energy producers-- not the heavy taxes and regulations presently working against our oil industry. More jobs will be created if our oil industry is at least treated fairly, if not incentivized by the government. The Keystone XL pipeline will also create more jobs.

As repeated above, more jobs and higher wages, translates to less crime in America which in turn reduces the need for police!

Present government policies put environmental protection above America's need for energy and jobs

Lately it has become obvious that the executive branch of government is against the oil industry in general on the misguided theory that oil drilling and operations are somehow bad for the environment. Apparently the environment is more important than American people who need jobs and Americans who don't want to be at the mercy of OPEC for their oil and energy needs. Somehow through the ingenuity and perseverance of American entrepreneurs and oil companies, America now has a chance to become energy independent despite the hostility of the government against our oil drilling owners and workers.

It is vitally important that our own oil industry flourishes and provides jobs for Americans. Oil is also vital to our military and it is dangerous to depend on OPEC sources if a major war breaks out in the Middle East.

Summary

Present government policies are anti-business and are poor for growth of the American economy and job creation. So-called "free trade" has damaged businesses and destroyed entire American industries. Illegal immigration is out of control. Tax rates on corporations are the highest in the world. The regulations on business have raised the cost of doing business and resulted in massive lay-offs of workers. The Federal Reserve

Board has virtually destroyed the real value of the dollar by printing massive amounts of money. The Environmental Protection Agency hampers energy companies, oil drilling operations, and new pipelines, causing the loss of jobs and cutting oil production that is needed to break the grip of the criminal OPEC countries on America. The minimum wage policy has caused loss of jobs and inflation over many decades. Military and welfare entitlement spending is out of control. Infrastructure decay is reaching dangerous proportions.

Chapter 8
Poverty and the conditions that can lead to increasing poverty and crime

Who are the People in Poverty?

When I mention poverty and the poor, do not think that I am speaking about a certain race. Poverty is present in all races. In fact I include people in the "poverty" group those who have been what people would usually refer to as the "middle class", and outwardly they still appear to be middle class, but who have not saved enough money to retire on. When they reach the usual retirement age of 65 these "middle class" people find they have to continue to work (if they are able), or they have to depend on Social Security, Medicare, Medicaid, and sometimes even welfare payments just to survive.

Poor Education

There are relationships between all of the above. For example, schools tend to be bad in poor areas and students from poor families often do not get proper nutrition and motivation to learn in school effectively. Bullying and gang activity do not help the education process. School security is poor and oftentimes kids are carrying weapons into schools. Learning standards and testing methods are inadequate. Classroom instruction is often interrupted by bad behavior of students causing discipline problems.
Poor education tends to continue the poverty cycle into the next generation and it is part of the reason for unemployment in the poor sections of the country.

Poor Nutrition

Poor nutrition, drug use, smoking, and alcohol abuse in the poor communities can lead to sickness that eventually requires medical attention.
Children do poorly in school without proper nutrition. So, poor nutrition can lead to even

worse poverty when children drop out of school and cannot get work that pays enough to live on. As the children grow up without a good education, they can fall into the trap of drugs and the drug culture, prostitution, and crime.

Crime results mainly from poverty

Poverty and drug use is one of the drivers of crime. Crime is costly to the victims and the communities. More police are required to maintain order and more prison cells are needed to detain criminals. The cost of crime continues to rise as drug cartels expand and more people use illegal drugs. The number of police and the power of police continue to grow as the "war on drugs" and the population of the poor increases.

How Many People Live in Poverty?

In the U.S. alone more than 16% lived in poverty in 2012. The government definition of people living in poverty is an income less than $23,050. The actual number of people in poverty is estimated to be approximately 43.6 million including 20% of American children. Approximately 643,000 people are homeless in the U.S. The above statistics can be found at the following link no. 49.

Link. 49.

http://en.wikipedia.org/wiki/Poverty_in_the_United_States

What Group Receives the Most in Entitlements?

You may be surprised to learn that almost every economic sector of the U.S. population receives a portion of government entitlement benefits. In fact the middle class (60% of the population) receives 58% of the total, whereas the poor (20% of the population according to the data) receive about 32% of the entitlements. The top 20% income level, receive 10 % of the entitlements. It is true that the poor receive more in proportion to their population then the middle class. But according to the data on the link below, the middle class and the top 20% income levels receive 68% of the entitlements. This data is from the Washington Post in an article by Brad Plumer. See the following link no. 50:

Link 50.
http://www.washingtonpost.com/blogs/wonkblog/wp/2012/09/18/who-receives-benefits-from-the-federal-government-in-six-charts/

Now the question is: Why should the middle class and the upper income people receive more of the entitlement pie than the poor class?

Part of the answer is that the Social Security System and Medicare require people to pay into the SS and Medicare "funds" as a deduction from their paychecks. So in theory everyone who has such deductions taken out of their pay, is due benefits when they reach retirement age, regardless of their net worth, there income level, or even if they continue working.

In actuality the money paid by workers currently employed is used to pay Social Security and Medicare benefits for people that are already retired. So a worker who pays into these welfare systems does not really build a fund for his own use. Therefore, there is no guarantee that the worker working now will ever get any benefits when he retires, and he probably will not if the system is broke or there is an economic collapse. Some of the middle class and upper class people know how to "work the system to get as many government benefits as they can. Another reason the middle class and upper class get so much in entitlements is that a good portion of these people are elderly, disabled, or both.

Look at the data from the above link. The entitlement pie is split up further as follows:

53% goes to people age 65 and up (the Social Security program is not properly funded.)
20% goes to disabled non-elderly
18% goes to working households, non-disabled and non-elderly

9% goes to miscellaneous persons.

Now there is generally no question that the elderly and the disabled should get entitlement benefits *if they are in need*, and we might assume that the working households that receive benefits are the people in poverty.

Are there any groups in the above list you can stop paying entitlements to? The answer is obviously no to that question. Is there fraud in the system? Certainly, but it takes a lot of investigative work to find it. That means that the government will most likely have to hire additional people to do the investigations.

Conclusion: Entitlements cannot be cut out totally for any group and as the population grows the entitlement payments required to maintain reasonable standards of living will only increase. Of course it is possible that the entitlement payments could be reduced, but what politician in Washington DC will be willing to take the punishment for suggesting any cuts?

How Much Money Does the Government Spend on Entitlements?

The federal budget for the year 2013 is as follows (data from the link below):

Total spending	$6.2T
Pensions	$1.1T

Health	$1.1T
Education	$0.8T
Defense	$0.9T
Welfare	$0.7T

T stands for trillions.

If we separate out the entitlement spending from the above list (assuming there are no entitlements included in the Education and Defense budgets), we have the total entitlement spending of $2.4 trillion, or approximately 46.8% of the budget. The present population of the U.S. is about 316 million people (see The Population Clock below.)
So if the total budget is $6.2T, the amount of money spent per person is approximately $19.62, and the entitlement spending portion per person is approximately $7.59 per year. This does not sound like a lot of money but there is a net one person growth every 13 seconds in the U.S. (see The Population Clock below.) So the entitlement expenditures will have to keep growing and growing, becoming a larger and larger portion of the budget. See the following link 51 for the government spending data:

Link 51.
http://www.usgovernmentspending.com/

What is the National Debt?

The U.S. national debt is close to $17 trillion and growing quickly. See the link below to the USA Debt Clock.com. There are also a lot of unfunded U.S. liabilities such as Social Security that is $15.2 trillion and growing. The Medicare unfunded liability is an unbelievable $79.2 trillion and growing. The total unfunded liabilities- per- household is over $1 million. Basically, unless your household has assets over $1 million, you would be busted if you had to pay your share of the money the U.S. government owes.

It is true that theoretically, a government is an entity with an infinite lifetime and therefore the National Debt never has to be re-paid. Of course the problem is that the government does have to pay the interest on the Treasury bonds that it has issued that comprises the major part of the National Debt.

Now if the government has plenty of revenue coming in to pay the interest on the Treasury bonds (and enough revenue to cover its other obligations) then there is not an immediate problem. But if times get tough and tax revenue declines due to high unemployment and business bankruptcies, there might not be enough money to cover the Treasury bond interest payments because of entitlements, military, and other more pressing obligations.

Once it becomes known that the government can no longer make interest payments or make good payments of the face value of T-bonds at maturity, there will be a terrible crash of Treasury bonds and a rush to sell out the bonds. The T-bond crash will affect banks world-wide as well as the treasuries of countries that hold T-bonds.

Major Countries That Hold Large Quantities of U.S. Treasury Securities

The link below gives a list of a large number of countries that own U.S. securities such as T-bonds and T-bills. I only mention a few major countries here. The data is as of March 2013:

China $1.25 trillion
Japan $1.10 trillion
Brazil $258.6 billion
Switzerland $184.2 billion
Russia $162.5 billion
UK $150.6 billion

If the U.S. gets in the position that it cannot support its debt, it will be a terrible economic collapse that will affect the entire world! See Link 52:

Link 52.
http://www..gov/resource-center/data-chart-center/tic/Documents/mfh.txt

Will the U.S. Ever Reduce the National Debt and Balance the Budget?

How can the U.S. ever catch up to its obligations and reduce the national debt, of $17 trillion, when its revenue is only $2.7 trillion a year, and it is spending 2.3 times its revenue? With the present partisan politics and the massive growing entitlements it does not seem possible that the national debt or the budget expenditures will be controlled any time soon.
Until the government gets control of its finances by balancing the budget and starting to reduce the national debt, there is a danger that people will loss confidence in the capability of the U.S. to meet its obligations.
The value of the dollar will drop even further with inflation increasing steadily.
When there is a crisis of confidence, it is easy for a rumor or some disaster to trigger a panic and a crash in the stock market, and other financial institutions such as banks.
The following link no. 53 shows the real time values of the national debt and the U.S. unfunded liabilities.

Link 53.
http://usadebtclock.com/

Will There Be a Loss of Confidence in the U.S. ?

If people loose their trust in Treasury bonds and the U.S. government itself, it could trigger a crash in the bond market. A crash in the bond market will trigger a collapse of many large and small banks because a major portion of their capital assets are held in bonds.

If taxes are not increased or no new sources of revenue are developed, or spending is not significantly reduced to have a balanced budget, the government keeps going further and further into debt. The government may be forced to cut vital services such as our defense forces and intelligence resources, leaving us at the mercy of terrorists and rogue countries!

This is the road to becoming a third-world country and economic collapse.

Entitlements will keep increasing as the population keeps growing and aging at the same time. The military and discretionary budgets will get squeezed more and more by the entitlements budget until the U.S. government is no longer a world power and the country will lose control of law and order. The end result will be chaos, economic collapse, a massive increase in crime, and finally the creation of a dictatorial police state that has all powers and grants little if any freedom.

The Population Clock

The population of the U.S. will continue to increase and without an improvement of government policies to reduce poverty and crime, the amount of crime will increase forcing heavy population jurisdictions to increase their police forces, and the power of the police will inevitably increase.

See the following link no. 54 for the U.S. and world population clock.

Link 54.
http://www.census.gov/popclock/

The Economic Effects on Poverty

The state of the economy always has an effect on the poverty rate. In a bad economy, there are generally fewer jobs available and the pay will generally not be as good as in a good prosperous economy. Of course we already know that the fewer jobs that are available and the lower the pay, the more the crime rate will increase. So, a good economy is a prime requisite for low crime. If the economy is bad we can usually lay the blame on federal government policies or an incompetent Federal Reserve Board, or both. Our economy has really been less than it could be for decades because of the government regulations and over-taxation of businesses, especially small business.

If the government would only see the light and make the U.S. a friendly place for businesses to form, grow and prosper, we would have a lot more and better paying jobs available for workers. It would reduce poverty tremendously by both creating jobs and reducing the need for welfare entitlements.

1. Mortgages

There are many effects of poverty on the economy. The last almost disastrous effect in the 2007 – 2009 economic crisis was a glut of low quality mortgages that the government approved for low income people that should not have been approved. These mortgages were issued to people who at a later date could not meet their payments because of a slumping economy and many job layoffs at the time.

The low-grade mortgages were packaged in blocks and sold as securities by banks and other financial institutions as if they were sound investments. Unfortunately, the securities contained good as well as bad mortgages. The entire banking system was contaminated with these securities and no one knew what value could be placed on them. A lack of confidence in banks developed and added to the economic instability at the time. As of early 2013, banks are still trying to get rid of the contaminated mortgage securities.

So who was at fault? The government was mainly at fault for approving sub-standard quality mortgages that people were not really qualified for financially. Many home foreclosures occurred when people lost their jobs or had financial set-backs of some kind.

By approving these sub-standard mortgages the government was actually causing the home buyers more harm than good when eventually they lost their homes due to foreclosure. This kind of activity by the government has started again. We never seem to learn from past mistakes.

Also at fault were the financial brokers on Wall Street who packaged the failing mortgages into the collateralized mortgage obligations (CMO's) and sold them to various institutions as supposedly good investments. See the following link no. 55 for information on CMO's:

Link 55.
http://en.wikipedia.org/wiki/Collateralized_mortgage_obligation

There are two major government agencies that approve or finance mortgages. They are the FHA, and FNMA. The following are links nos. 57 and 58 that give information on the work of these agencies:

Link 57.
http://www.zillow.com/fha-loan/

Link 58.
http://homeguides.sfgate.com/fannie-mae-loan-2036.html

The government also has a new program called HARP (Home Affordable Mortgage Program.) It appears that the same mistakes made before the financial crisis of 2008, are being made all over again. Will another wave of bad mortgages and home foreclosures hit like it did in 2008-2009 and contribute to the next economic downturn or be enough to even trigger a financial collapse? The answer is yes, in all likelihood. HARP is an example of the what lengths the liberal "do-gooders" are will to go to, supposedly helping poor people, when in fact they are setting up an economic time bomb that will risk another disastrous downturn that will just make poor people even more destitute, and cause a lot of the lower middle class people to fall below the poverty line.

Don't liberal politicians know what the "unintended consequences" are going to be resulting from their "liberal" programs such as HARP? Or do they know and don't care? Maybe all they are interested in is making political points for their re-election at the expense of the poor they are supposedly helping?

High U.S. labor costs.

The U.S. has some of the highest labor rates in the world. Why? It is because of the greedy and self-destructive desire of labor for higher and higher wages, and the extreme liberal politicians who support labor's demands, and the so-called "minimum wage." Don't misunderstand me. I am not against labor or labor unions and labor should be able to earn enough to live a good life. But too much is too much, and we are pricing our labor out of the world market.

What if our labor costs our higher than other countries? It would be ok if the U.S. was self sufficient in all commodities and could produce all of our own needs without any imports of goods. But this is not the case. The U.S. imports much more than it exports. The U.S. has lost many major industries to overseas companies.

For example we have lost a great textile industry, consumer electronics (audio-visual entertainment products, cell phones, toys, etc.) Much of our steel industry has been eliminated by cheaper import steel products. The U.S. automobile industry struggles against cheaper automobiles from Japan, Korea, and China imported by the millions and manufactured in the U.S. under foreign control with massive amounts of money flowing to the foreign companies headquartered overseas.

Summary

Government entitlement spending and the national debt is out of control, while poverty, poor education, and poor nutrition is leading to more and more crime. High U.S. labor costs have made the U.S. unable to compete in industrial markets resulting in the loss of entire industries and jobs. An increasing population and no improvement in jobs is resulting in more crime and an increasing police force with more police power. The number of police and the power of police continues to grow as the "war on drugs" and the population of the poor increases. Bad economic conditions resulting from bad government polices generate poverty. A crisis of confidence in the U.S. dollar and treasury bonds could result in a major financial disaster and chaos bringing about the conversion of the American democracy into a police dictatorship.

www.ingramcontent.com/pod-product-compliance
Lightning Source LLC
Chambersburg PA
CBHW031629210526
45464CB00004B/1812